my personal stories

Roberta Markbreit

INKWATER PRESS

PORTLAND • OREGON
INKWATERPRESS.COM

Scan this QR Code to learn more about this title

Cover and interior design by Emily Coats

Publisher: Inkwater Press

Paperback
ISBN-13 978-1-62901-151-6 | ISBN-10 1-62901-151-7

Printed in the U.S.A.
All paper is acid free and meets all ANSI standards for archival quality paper.

1 3 5 7 9 10 8 6 4 2

Contents

The safe entry of my generation into adulthood came because of the sacrifices of those who came before us.

Becoming Home

To Endure

KNOWING JULIUS BROUGHT INTO SHARP FOCUS A COMMENT MADE TO my parents by the husband of friends who often traveled:

"New Yorkers cannot see beyond the Hudson River."

He was our pioneer, the first on our block to become suburban. His house is across the street, catty-corner from ours, on the end of the block, at the curb a short distance from the side of Highland Elementary School. He boasted about the early days, a mere nine months before we arrived, being alone on an empty graveled road, trekking every day to the mailbox a block away, on the curb of the stilled boulevard, Crawford Avenue. Just before we came, he watched the final addition of the school go up. Also before we moved in, his front lawn had been laid down without the interference of a sidewalk, keeping the desired aura of country living intact.

He strode down our driveways, advising on installations of sod and plumbing; offering insights on innovative modern items we had never heard of, such as separate spray faucets set into the upper corners of kitchen sinks and vacuum cleaners set permanently into walls with portable tubes that could be carried up and down the stairs. More than once, there was a visit at the front door, his dark eyes boyishly ominous at the prospect of a ticket being slipped under the windshield wiper of our car, now parked the wrong way on the street, while he pointed to it as we looked to view it through the front window.

On one particular afternoon, he came to our door and announced that he had ordered four valuable pin oak trees from Kentucky.

"Pin oaks don't often last here," he went on, "so the deal was easy to get, cheap and worth it." A broad smile emerged.

Summer had just begun. After dinners, we stood barefoot on the smooth cement of the driveway, feeling prosperous and humble at the same time, savoring the length of it as owners of our own home. And then, looking all the way down to the curb with satisfaction, our eyes rose irresistibly across the street to the corner house and its lush front lawn, barren of a typical sidewalk, unlike any other.

One day, we looked up from whatever we were doing--pulling weeds, mowing, or just walking to our cars to start our errands--when the truck from Kentucky appeared on the center of the street. Gathered on the curbsides, we stared at the unfamiliarity of it, dusty and dented. Dwarfed by its size, Julius was already there alongside it, beckoning us to come over, waving his hand toward his chest.

"C'mon, c'mon." he encouraged us in his raspy voice.

We congregated around while he swept up easily onto the running board, grasping the upper rim of the open window, leaning at us joyfully.

"You can take what you want! Take your time!" he exuded, waving us closer to the back of the pickup.

So, we each pointed at random, saying, "I'll take that one." Or, "The far one hiding on the other side." And, finally, as if it were compelling us to choose it, we said, "This one closest to us."

Where to put it, the tree we never asked for? In the backyard seemed best.

The snaky tentacles of its root system had formed into an enormously monstrous bulb. It would take at least three strong men to put it into the ground. None of us could even budge it. So, the answer seemed to be to ask Mike, the professional landscaper of our block, to do what he did best.

Mike and his men set it into the ground with a purity of love for the earth that we will never know. He dug, patted, smoothed, working his shovel or rake backward and forward, caressing in his own manly way, a gentle man, precise and patient.

Settled deeply inside the dank, moist soil, just off-center on the right, catty corner to the small pear tree on the left that was set against the bushes and behind the jungle gym, its tiny leaves gave trickles of momentary shade; then they lifted into the high heat of the upswept summer winds, a show of acclimation to its new permanent home. It filled our yard with promise.

Slowly, slowly, one year after the other, the bark grew thick and hard; the branches reached like dancers' limbs in search of perfect pose. In autumn, the leaves curled and crackled and faded to cinnamon; in winter, the gray bark and limbs stiffened and grew black, and crackled, too; in spring, dots of nubile green buds tantalized; in summer, the leaves slowly bloomed a deepened green, their prickly shapes with thread-like veins emerging.

Out in front, there were our other young, yearning trees: the sunburst honey locust alongside the curb; the pink flowering crab in the center of the lawn; and the leafy purple plum in front of the two widely-spread windows.

Across the street and down two houses on the right, Roger smoked his after-dinner cigars in front of his house from the very beginning. Savoring the summer air from the curb of our driveway, we were bemused by the bliss reflected in the length of time of his standing there, smoke gliding across his heavy eyelids. As if startled by our presence, he turned to us with a dreamy smile, then held the cigar aloft and tapped it so that the stub of ash fell, crashing to the ground in silence. He crossed the street, his slippers scraping the cement, and came to meet us at the curb.

"What's new?" he wanted to know.

"Not much."

"How's business?"

"All right," we murmured; in unison, we nodded. "And yours?"

Rocking back a little, confidently lifting the cigar to his lips, the answer was obvious. His cheeks caved in and puffed out, and in a gentlemanly manner, he raised his chin so that the abrupt, chugging puffs of heavy smoke bypassed our faces.

"How's your pin oak?" he wanted to know.

"Good. Fine. What about yours?"

"Not so good. Less than perfect."

Our eyes darted across the street. Close to the curb in front of his house, its tiny faded leaves were drooping just a bit. I felt sorry for the tree.

"Maybe you're doing something wrong."

"What do *you* do to *yours*?"

"We just let it grow. Mike watches it."

"H-m-m," and back he turned to cross the street toward home, his slippers spewing soft friction once again.

Helen, Roger's wife, bought gadgets to save their tree. Into its root system she inserted a periscope-like tube that was supposed to take all the alien elements out, and put good, healthy juice in. She even put up small ropes around it to isolate it from whatever elements she imagined were its enemies. Last summer, just a couple of weeks after she finally gave up, it gave up, too, and died.

The two others died, as well, even the one that Julius chose. Boldly, he had his tree planted across the boundary line of his lot so that half of it belonged to the next-door neighbors, giving them an unexpected privilege. He pretended confidence, then indifference; and, finally, out of exasperation or impatience, he robbed it of its chance to try to live. Without our knowing, it was pulled from the earth, carried away, and one autumn day, we noticed it was gone.

Yet ours was different. As its limbs, over time, yearned toward our bedroom window, my soul grew with our tree, so that, as its leaves reached closer, facing me, slowly bulging, being green and turning gold and yellow and cinnamon and then green again, I longed to reach through and touch them.

Mike waited at the front door. He asked that we follow him to the backyard. He walked deliberately to the tree, pointed one at a time to small black spots inside the ridges of the bark.

"Enemies," he declared softly. "It, too, might die. Pin oaks are not native to Illinois and it is always risky to force them to adapt here."

Oh, no!! Not *our* tree, so full of life.

The sun brightened the yard. We stood close to Mike as, with instinctive patience, he plugged iron nails into holes we had never noticed, where parasites, following their own natures, had made paths to come and go.

Each morning, now, I wake to the life of our pin oak tree. I am ever discovering it. It has the grace of a strong ballerina, branches lyrical, stretching wide and far, its shape a simple triangle, like the Christmas tree cards I cut from green colored paper when I was growing up.

Each autumn and winter, I watch as the leaves, one by one, begin to fall and drift away, and I wait for the very last to sail and disappear into the swooping wind and cold, which, to my astonishment, happens just a moment before Spring arrives. Winter has been here for some time now, and I can still find, every now and then, a fragile curled leaf dancing lightly on the surface of new, thick snow, making the whiteness even brighter just before dusk. And when I look up, to see how many more are left, I find leaves turned like limp hands, their stems clinging strongly to the branches.

The children's play set has rusted, birds now scooting in and out of the hollow crossbar overhead. The bushes surrounding it have now matured; the grass is now deeply green and thick. With our neighbors we have turned the soil of two empty lots behind our house into a garden before the owners snatch them back and crunch our cucumbers and tomatoes and celery with noisy bulky machines that flatten the land for constructing houses for sale.

Our tree has soared higher than the roof, and, from my window, I crane my neck to see it.

The First Visit

I SEE THE IMAGE OF MY MOTHER SITTING IN HER SPRAWLING CHAIR, alone in her new, smaller apartment, smoking a cigarette, her arm draped heavily down its long wide rim.

She was excited at our coming, so much so that she gazed from her window, high above, waiting, and saw us as we parked and strolled toward her building. It must have been ages for her because we spent several minutes parking just so in a very difficult spot.

While cups clinked and the coffee's muffled bubbles boiled, the few of us laughed heartily with her over the voluptuous breakfast she had prepared for us: her own special eggs, scrambled soft and fluffy to a fresh yellow, hot so that the string of steam rose in the small traditionally burnt pan as she shoved it quickly back and forth over the burner, then turned them upside down quickly onto the white serving plate; deep orange-colored lox already splayed out like shiny petals, the delicate white veins seeming to palpitate; plain and onion and egg bagels in a basket, yellow and pale and burnt brown; a block of cream cheese, its pure white top fresh with scattered dew, on a little flowered butter plate; a slender, solid stick of unsalted butter nearby on a matching dish; a heavy glass pitcher of regular milk; home-made orange juice, already filled in glasses to the right above our plates from a crystal pitcher now set over a favorite tablecloth patterned in large flowers, its soft colors faded.

The oval dining room table facing the living room and its matching chairs with black leather seats seemed misplaced in the corner alongside the tiny kitchen. It belonged in my memory of when the stylish set was new, a blend of traditional and contemporary cherry wood. Then, we had just moved into the first of Chicago's modern skyscraper apartment buildings, all by itself on the corner of Belmont Avenue and the Outer Drive, with large green tiles up and down the front of it. The entire wall of the large living room and the dining area next to it was made of glass, facing the lake, giving us a sweeping view.

The coffee pot bubbling softly kept our laughter buoyant. We wanted to cheer my mother, so recently widowed, and to boost the necessity of her having to move. We talked incessantly about the intelligence of her choice. The powerful presence of my father lingered.

Looking down from the high bay windows over the street and the miraculous view of the lush tops of trees, and to the left, several blocks away, the rooftop I had never seen of the building that I grew up in, it all pleased me, for that is the history that my mother and I know, and the loss of the vast view of the lake was strangely comforting.

Her new apartment is so light and cheery. Her effort to have everything placed in it a reflection of the past eighteen years along the Outer Drive was in the air, as though she had gently tapped the tops of furniture just before we came: the baby grand piano inside the window on the right that looked out upon grand residences on Hawthorne Place; squat chairs designed in yellow harlequin fabric, facing one another in front of the middle window, picked out and insisted upon by my father, making the decorator and my mother cringe; and, a tall, button-stuffed Victorian chair, originally pale blue taffeta, now, olive green velvet, and somehow prized as an heirloom.

How odd to be settled on this street. It belonged to the leader of our crowd from my grammar school life. She lived down the way, two houses off Broadway, in a fifteen-room brick home with a cement porch in front and a small ballroom on the third floor where we had boy-girl parties. There was a swing set in the back, and I used to see how high I could soar, feeling giddy and daring. It is still there, occupied by strangers now, making it not hers anymore, unjustly so.

Then I remembered more. Here we were reveling inside a tall, modern glass and black steel building with sharp, flat edges and windows that were shaded like sunglasses, where a lovely, white-painted home with a wraparound porch with pillars on either side of it used to be. Our friend knew the boy who lived here, a pale quiet boy with slick brown hair that fell straight over one eyebrow, shielding his serious, self-conscious facial expression, his brown eyes always downward.

The sun pushed through the windows, its brightest of the day, and we became restless; then, intoxicated with its heady wine and we were drunk from it, wanting to climb the walls or take off and fly. Our gaiety rose. We did not want to leave.

"We're going, Mom," Jerry said, for all of us, with a soft apology.

"Oh--all right," my mother answered, too quickly, at the lowest ebb of the day.

Back down on the street, we saw things we never see in the suburbs: old women—widows—in long navy gabardine coats walking arm in arm on the warm, crackling pavements; a young father pushing his baby twins swiftly in a stroller while, dressed identically, their little white-bonneted heads flopped onto their chests.

The sun healed and caressed us. We strolled to our car, turning our heads to see the same, oldest of trees and homes on the street that I knew as a youth.

Impulsively, I turned back, my whole body stretching to see which window was hers. We all stopped, and counted up, but missed. Again. Nearer, but not exactly. Again. Oh, yes, there she is, there she is, waving, her hand flapping sturdily for us to see. My heart leaped way up to her. I waved, faster and faster, all the way up to the fourteenth floor, inside the frame of trees and sky, 'way, 'way up to the corner of the smoked bay window. Her figure stood sturdy, full, real within the mist. She would be the last to turn away. Her face looked so small, 'way, 'way up there. But her smile was unmistakable.

Butch

There was the gentle pull on my braid. I had been looking down aimlessly into the glass case, my cheeks warm from the glow of the lights fanning up from under the staged shelves so that the reflection looking back at me from the counter was distorted like a Modigliani portrait: my face absurdly long, my elongated eyes almond-shaped with eerie curved shadows beneath my bottom lids. Even before I turned around, I knew. I held back, giving one last inane glance into the overly glaring rows of absurdly bulky, overpriced handbags.

I looked up, my eyes gleaming from the sophisticated fluorescence all around, sparking the blush on my face of a teenage girl's hidden yearning. It was Butch, smiling down at me, waiting, dressed in a navy blue blazer and a pale blue dress shirt with the buttoned down collar ruffled a bit, his large shoulders sensuous in their patience. I saw the young love that lingered in his fixed brown eyes.

OH! NO! The shiny black silk hair with the suave wave on top was gone! Instead, there were flat dark patches above his ears.

But then, there was the long dark face, its expression wanting understanding; the long nose, and, as ever, his thinly lashed eyelids closed halfway, emitting his own unique blend of arrogance and self-effacement.

Before I could catch myself, a flirtatious smile erupted.

"Oh—BUTCH--." I was holding back and flooding forward, all at once. "It's--YOU! I can't believe it--. Here--."

Flowered dresses tightly fitted on mannequins in stiff poses; umbrellas hung on posts scattered all around; blouses lined on hanging racks--all were swirling along with the fluorescent lights in the background. I glanced down at the hardness of the vast floor to steady myself; but, instead, its brass chips were like the Milky Way winking right back at me and swirling, too. And, so, I gave way to floating, being swept away even more.

I looked up to see his boyish smile stilled and genuine, never having changed. He swept forward and his massive arms enveloped me within the warmth of his flannel blazer as he pressed my cheek beneath his shoulder, forcing my eyelids closed and my nose pressed into the soft folds.

"Mmphf!" he grunted.

It was but a moment, timeless.

Maid

Rosalee is tall and very thin, except in the middle, where, under her long green wraparound cotton housedress with the colorful flowers patterned all over it, her body mushrooms like a soft, heavy cloud. Her deep black eyes are centered with tiny dots that glimmer and there are thin erratic eyebrows that half-circle above them. (I wonder if Rosalee has painted them onto her shiny, unwrinkled face; I try to imagine her at home, in bed, without any eyebrows at all.) Her black hair ends at the nape of her neck in curly strands like a cap she has pulled tightly over her head and it wiggles like spaghetti as she talks and moves. Her mouth is filled with large white teeth, interspersed with chunks of gold. (That mouth, oh, that mouth, tells what it wants to tell. Mostly, it hides a storehouse of secrets. When Rosalee makes fun of my absent-mindedness, a loud, shrill laugh rolls over her tongue and bursts out between her full lips. I wonder if she means to be cruel, hiding anger or hostility, but, no, she's sweet once again.) Long smooth legs, tapered and skinny, just like her large feet; shoulders, large and bony; her chest flat and large, too.

But, oh, her skin, her beautiful, soft, shiny, caramel-brown skin! Sometimes I'll hug her on purpose, so I can touch it. It is smooth, like satin. I linger on her arm or her cheek, just to enjoy its velvetiness for another instant longer.

We hum along, I, at my studies; she, in another room, laughing loudly, on purpose, probing at a drawer, a photograph, a letter from my friend.

"Ha-a- - - ha-a-a-a!" she'll cry, with delight, so I'll be sure to hear.

I'm annoyed: My train of thought is interrupted. But--I want her to stay here, I want her to want this place, so I force my interest:

"What, Ro, what did you say? What's so funny?"

"Oh-h, nothin, honey."

And then, a racing forward of breathless, childish words:

"Oh, Dandy (our calico cat) an' Twinki (our black cat) are playin' an' fightin' an' rollin' over each other an' slid right into th' stairs, an' Dandy was abs'lootly stunned, honey. H-a-a, ha-a-a-a!"

I laugh almost as hard as she. We share this moment. We enjoy it, yes, we do.

"See Dandy peepin' roun' th' stairs? She's waitin' for Twinki, so she can give her one big smack!"

Then, in a loving, rushing, staccato whisper, so the sister-cats can't hear, but I can:

"See, see, see, honey, she's waitin' an' lookin'--! Oh, them cats uh mine are somethin' else, somethin' else!"

Sure enough, careless Twinki walks by, --and pounce--!! there's Dandy on her back, claws in Twinki's neck and legs around Twinki's thin belly. Cats, tails swinging sensuously, cautiously separate and the game is temporarily over.

"What'd Ah tell yuh, girl, don' Ah know mah babies?"

I wonder what's behind that smooth face, behind that storehouse of secrets. She was raised as an orphan, in, did she say, Virginia, or New York? She has a cousin somewhere in Virginia. She discovered a sister, (who doesn't resemble her at all) and a brother. Once in a while, she speaks of this brother, somewhere, somewhere. She travels to New York sometimes to visit this semblance of a family. All were reunited after years of separation.

She speaks of sister Margaret once in a while:

"Girl, that chil' can't (the t softened in her tone) get her lazy man to lose weight fer nothin'! She stays home, now, an' nurses that ailin' arm o' hers."

Rosalee lives in an apartment; she sleeps on a cot—alone. A set-up section of the dining room, the hub of the household, is her "private" bedroom. Her husband sleeps in the "real" bedroom; he's recently retired. He awkwardly, constantly, gets in her way, inconsiderately eating a cake she baked for herself, or unexpectedly bringing a friend home for dinner. Though she casts him off as an inconvenience, she honestly loves and needs him: Would she call him, "my man" in vain?

Rosalee, patient and self-contained, certainly doesn't represent today's modern, restless black women. Her people were slaves, just like theirs, but she doesn't resemble them at all. There were the three openly arrogant girls in Afros in the cafeteria who pushed me aside and laughed loudly, triumphant. And yet, the bright, soft-spoken, well-liked Head Start teacher invited me to a party at her home, setting aside her dialogue about white America. The gracious young woman in the Science laboratory who is of a bi-racial family easily and patiently helped me with experiments.

What *does* Rosalee think of the younger black culture? Given the new opportunities of today's youth, does she ache because of those possibilities newly dawned in society which never touched her, those that were forbidden to her?

Does her heritage plague her? I wonder: Is she angry? Is she ever sorry she was born? Does she think of herself as especially black? Yet, I don't think of her as "Afro-American."

At times, she's very sad. Then, she moves slowly and her voice is thick, raspy and heavy. That lovely mouth is closed and unwilling to give. She's lonely and her heart is heavy. She'll say, in answer to my query,

"Oh-h, no, nothin's wrong; I jus' ache an' my artha-ritis is actin' up again, an' that man o'mine makes me <u>want to kill</u>, I swear."

Her mouth twists and curls, and two long thin lines between her brows form the semblance of a frown. Even then, her mouth is firm and smooth and beautiful. I love her then, especially.

We'll pass this day together. I want to help her heal; I want her to forget this incident that reminds her of the many lonely circumstances in her life. I'll ask,

"Do you think I should cook the brisket all day, or only four hours?"

(I've cooked for years, but I'm now in need of help.)

"What's wrong with our iron, Ro? Only you can fix it right."

Ten minutes later,

"Ro, your program is on; don't you want to watch it?"

A rush of meaningless words, but she reluctantly turns it on. I ache for her.

Long ago, when I tried to weather a crisis that threatened to destroy me, she told me strongly, urgently, firmly,

"Oh-h, when Ah wuz very young, Ah couldn' see no way out. Ah thought tha' other people were surely more important than Ah wuz; people an' life were all aroun' me, gettin' me down. Then, yuh know wha', honey, Ah said to mahself,

'Aw, *no one* is worth killin' mahself for. They're not gonna get *me* to the point where they can say they've done me in. No one in this whol' wide worl' is as important as *me*. Ah'm jus' as good as anyone else.'

"An' honey, evah since then, Ah've always known tha's no lie: Ah'm as good as *anyone*."

She laid her voice heavily on *any-one*, like she always does on a final word, to stress a point. (I strongly agreed with her on this.)

"Rosalee, you're *better than most people.*"

Rosalee is honest in her judgments. She came to me with a newspaper photograph that showed a burglar being led away by policemen. This man was tough, huge, and black, his frown deeply burrowed, his eyes, incredibly cold and mean.

"Honey," she said, "jus' look a' tha' man. Umh. A man like tha' has no heart, no feelin'. He's jus' pla-ain mean. Jus' think uh wha' a life he's led, to make him so hard. He'll never find wha' life is all about that way, tha's for sure! Um-huh, I wouldn' wan' to know him, ever! A man like tha' is sad, indeed!"

Does she long for luxury? Perhaps. She saved for a year to buy a lovely outfit that she saw in a store window near the elevated terminal. She saves for many such "luxuries:"

"The man," the owner of the shop, "knows wha' Ah like, an' always saves somethin' he knows Ah can't resist. Ah walk by, he rushes to the street, an' sez,

'Miz Morgan, we have an outfit yu'r gonna love. It wuz made jus' for you. It came in tuhday. Ah can make one up in y'ur size in no time.'

"Sure enough, Ah'll start payin' fer it that very day."

And everyone along the bus route knows Rosalee. Margaret, her sister, confided that Rosalee's popularity is high all along the daily workday route in which she travels. She tells me that the manager of the terminal coffee shop greets her sister as she opens the door:

"'How you feelin', Miz Morgan; you been sick?? Ah mist ya these past few weeks.' "

And the bus driver comments as, bundled up, shivering, she climbs the steps:

" 'How you doin' today? Yeh, it sure is cold enough.' "

Evelyn, the unsmiling grumpy neighbors' maid who regularly rides the train part of the way with her, sends a friendly wave as they separate to start their day across the street from one another. (Why does Rosalee entertain her presence with someone so unlike her?)

At the end of a day, as she readies to go home, I feel threatened as she unexpectedly quibbles about her forty cents for carfare, "forgetting" that I save her that forty cents (and the extra time it takes to ride the shuttle) by driving her to the train. (Why the meaningless treachery? A defense against the imbalance of life?)

My mother-in-law told me that in the very beginning, when Rosalee answered her ad for hiring a cleaning lady, she arrived for the interview in a yellow suit and a lace blouse, golden bracelets clicking away, her long slender fingers and long, strong nails painted dark red.

"I was mesmerized. She was all dressed up in finery, a real lady. I don't know what made me hire her. I must have seen her potential, that she would be the right person for our family."

Rosalee *became the family.*

My quest to find her essence, her soul, has become intricate and fascinating. There is her strength: the pure simplicity of her dignity; her no-nonsense, unforgiving standards; her proud, enduring need for sustenance from her family.

And then there is the unabashed slyness that juts out, as if she is not aware of it showing, and I am face-to-face with the nakedness of her instinctive trickery.

But, in the end, she is here with me, my loving friend.

Unexpected Visitors

THE YOUTHFUL, JUBILANT SALESMAN APPEARED ON THE FRONT STOOP, a clipboard set in the crook of his elbow, flat against his white wrinkled dress shirt, sleeves rolled up to his elbows, twirling a pencil between his fingers.

He was selling magazines for the future of America. He and his generation would someday inherit the leadership of our country, upholding the ideals of a just society, he enlightened me. I gave an instinctive glance to my right, which revealed his friend in a stance at the end of our driveway, feet apart, expressionless.

In order to do that, he continued, his gray eyes direct and unwavering, his generation needed to further their educations. And that is why he was here, he emphasized. Selling magazines door-to-door is in the true tradition of what has made our country great, the most earnest and the purest form of income that students like he could embrace. He had full expectations that his success would provide needed income to pay for university tuition and supplies.

Mine became the last, most recent signature at the very bottom of a long hand-written list, I noted, as I revealed my name, address and telephone number and the amount needed for subscribing to a year of magazine issues I had never thought to read, such as, "Psychology Today," and "Soldier of Fortune." I added, "Jack and Jill" to my choices because it felt vaguely familiar (and thus comforting) as I remembered occasionally glancing into the pages of this scholarly childhood magazine as I was growing up. And more, it reminded me of sitting on a bench in the audience while watching my cousin act in the "Jack and Jill Players Theater Group" when we were eight years old.

The telephone on the kitchen wall rang just as I came back inside over the threshold, after closing the door and cautiously monitoring through the front window the receding figures of the two salesmen, watching them stop and hesitate at the curb at a distance from the front of the house across the street. It was Bernice, calling from her house three doors down atop a little hill at the corner of the north end of the block. Her mannish voice was flat but urgent--a bit excited--unusually so, as she was generally calm. She warned me that young strangers were going up to houses in the neighborhood and selling magazines and I better not buy anything they were offering. They were phonies, she explained.

Soon after, three young adult Mormons arrived at our front door. Pale, smiling, in black skirts and trousers and white shirts and blouses, their bibles were tucked inside their elbows, their postures straightened with pure confidence, their eyes clear and steady.

I came out onto the stoop while they stayed on the driveway, looking up at me. I wanted to be kind, so I smiled as they spoke gently, offering me their faith and spirituality. I had never met such people. With their simple and honest pureness of speech and dress they seemed so out of place in the environment of the new suburbia of rough brick and flat unbroken cement and contrived lawns of solid green. As the sun baked down upon them, their earnest manner endured quietly, beseeching me to believe.

One of them handed me a pamphlet. I glanced at it, uncomfortable about the alien style of the drawing with its ancient religious pillars and faded yellow colorations. With genuine smiles they promised to come back next week. Satisfied, they walked away and turned the corner to the south, the side of Highland School in the background, with its smooth dark red brick and wide line of upright rectangular windows. I noticed the subtle dampness on the backs of their wrinkled shirts and blouses and the weariness of their trousers and long skirts.

They kept their promise. Back they came, week after week. They offered me (and I accepted) pamphlets entitled, "Word of Wisdom;" The Book of Abraham;" The Philosophical Basis of Mormonism." I enjoyed being with them. They were dedicated and serious, without guile; and at the same time, their eyes were bright and their faces flushed with the energy of youth.

"We are Jewish," I explained at last.

No matter. Predictably, they kept on coming, as if on time. I began to feel shamed because of a false, cordial encouragement that I knew would never come to fruition. They were working hard and I felt duplicitous, a thief, stealing their time and energy. It was hopeless: I would never be one of them.

Gradually, I hid from them my fascination with their courage and my need for adventure in knowing worlds other than my own. My conversations became merely courteous, my smile, frozen. They faded away, after that.

Then there were the wholesome, earnest, sweet-faced Girl Scouts, in well-pressed uniforms, all seemingly the same height, selling cookies (my favorites, peanut butter and crunchy sandwich); the eighth grade elementary students (boys and girls) of various complexions and heights selling gift wrapping paper two months before the winter holidays; the girls' and boys' high school basketball teams selling any item I could select (I, never having used nor craving any), colorfully photographed in the shiny pages of the brochures being flipped open in front of me: boxed sets of various dark jellies in octagonal jars; tall bulky tin cans of popcorn in various designs, each representing a different flavor such as caramel (my father's favorite), plain (my old-fashioned favorite), and cheddar cheese (my most un-favorite).

I delighted in the innocence of these young, unexpected visitors, their earnest faith in the sanctity of the adult world, their pure ambition. Even the older magazine sleazes fascinated me for their ability to tap into my naïve trust in what they had to say and, especially, their confident anticipation of my gullibility.

I was lonely and isolated in the newness of my daily life in the growing suburb, where trees were nubile and sidewalks smooth and unused, and where odd neighbors living close by were unenlightened and uninteresting. Amidst the vast emptiness abounding everywhere I looked, I missed the adventures of the city. I felt old.

At times, these vibrant children boosted my hope that I would embrace our new way of life that was supposed to bring ease and contentment to the new wave of a young generation of starry-eyed homeowners. For me, that never happened.

At the end of the Block: My Friend Bernice

LET ME TELL YOU ABOUT MY FRIEND BERNICE. SHE IS TALL AND SLENDER, with short dark hair and skin clear and as smooth as milk, with a small face, round brown eyes, a small nose and always a bright, red, cherry-painted mouth. The contrast is exceptionally striking. She sways as she walks. You would look twice if you saw her on the street or in any public place. Really, you *would* look twice.

Once I got beyond the surface, which is something she lets the few do whom she cares about, I found her beautiful, inside and out.

She is careful as she honors both my dignity and my faults. Yet she is not subservient. She is tenacious in her honesty, but her truths are not brutal, just truths. The respect she gives, she gets.

She is a loner like I, only it doesn't bother her as much as it has me. We are outsiders on the block, not at all like our neighbors, and we really do not like them very much, as we have nothing in common with them.

Once, she told me that she is afraid of everything in life, and that she sees "Indians lurking behind every tree."

When my father died she walked over to the kitchen door, opened it softly from the outside and stepped quietly in so as not to be awkward or intrusive. But her determination to console and her compassion for me who was only a neighbor back then took precedence. She knew precisely what to do and how to go about it. She stayed from morning until evening. Before my husband left, she whispered, aside to him,

"I'm going to stay with her."

From that day on, I would not let go of our friendship as I have of others, willingly. There are many things she's done since then to affirm my first impression.

I know she has her faults like the rest of us. No one is perfect. But her faults are so very minor, compared to her virtues.

I wish I could give her gifts to show my appreciation that a fine person such as she came into my life. Instead, I give complaints for her to listen to, and calls for help. That's what I give her.

But then, there is my friendship, my admiration and this tribute.

Away

Diary of Super Bowl XIX

For Jerry

THE CALL. IT WAS TO COME ON MONDAY MORNING, ACCORDING TO AN important staffer. The buildup was slow but energizing. There was a new kind of low-key pride in being in the background. As an alternate, he would be an experienced professional in a passive role, doing it with dignity.

The last time, there was the ultimate excitement. In 1983 the thrill was incredible: a swirling of unconfirmed rumors that melted into joyous truth, and once made public by the columnist revealing it on television, there was the whoosh of exuberant telephone calls from family and friends for his success at a young age.

The wait is always excruciating. There are the calls throughout the playoffs from the higher-ups and the officials sharing what they were told. Who made what? Who didn't? Consolation calls filled with longing. Elated congratulatory calls, but doubt and worry, just the same.

At home, for me, during the season, there is always the waiting. Unexpectedly, after a "controversial" call that I had not witnessed, there was a startling ringing of the telephone every few moments, in a kind of rhythm, with sportswriters in low, smirking tones making innuendoes; and mysterious voices spewing obscenities and ridicule. My fright grew to a peak, and, at last, I called the police station. I watched the officer stride up the driveway and I felt a bit relieved. The calls stopped. Was this a neighbor, watching?

Impulsively, I suspected who it might be. A fantasy erupted as I watched a brick fly through the air and crash through the large front window. I raged because of what I live with and wondered, even more, now, after so many years: Why?

At the beginning, there were all the poorly paid games on Sunday mornings at the football fields across the city, including Soldier Field, in the mud and rain. Inching forward, starting with grammar school, there was high school, college, the Big Ten, and now.

And then I remembered: In sunny California, in 1972, I saw what it meant to him. In the parking lot after the Rose Bowl game, he and a young man faced one another, their hands in their pockets of their trench coats, their feet solidly apart in a symmetry of understanding. I saw the purity of adoration in the bright eyes of the fan gazing up at him. And he, the Referee, looked back at him, just beyond his shoulder, satisfied and calm.

All week prior to the game, he, a man quiet about himself, ruminated. He was restless.

"Try to take it for what it is," I urged, carefully. "It's an honor. And relax, enjoy it; it will be an adventure."

The day before the flight, I began to panic. Our daughter called twice before nine in the morning, and talked leisurely. There were a million errands to run, and hardly time. I gritted my teeth with frustration (wanting to scream), but feigned interest.

He shopped for groceries. As soon as he came back, his arms full of small paper bags, I enthused about our getting away.

"When we get back home, you'll say, 'It was only for football, it's not a vacation,' " he blurted out, his hidden hurt feelings about my ongoing complaints finally spilling out.

"I'm looking *forward* to it," I protested.

There was the incessant ringing of the telephone all day long, mostly other officials calling with important business.

"I hope you don't have to go through this," he said to one from his own crew.

I stopped him in the kitchen. "Look at me," I insisted.

Gazing down at me, his brown eyes softened.

"I'm real proud of how you're handling this. Anyone can go out and be the hero. You're used to going forward, doing; you're an action person. This experience will enhance you; it's another facet of your career and it'll humble you. You'll be better for it."

He tried to interrupt my little speech with his own concurring comments but I stopped him halfway.

"That's why I've had this bad stomach for the past few days," he admitted earnestly.

We laughed, relieved, like children, and the tension broke.

There were more calls from our daughter.

"I'm lucky to have you for my mother," she told me. For the umpteenth time, I felt freshly surprised.

"I've <u>always</u> been glad you're my mother. You don't think so, but I am."

The morning of the flight to San Francisco, the tension came back. There was a big fight. I ruminated, like he said I would, about going. My slowness drove him nuts.

One of our cats, Max, knowing our leaving, urinated through the bedspread, sheets and mattress. Another, Dandy, got out, refused to budge from behind a stiff, winter-white hedge. In the backyard, still in our nightclothes, we cooed, coaxed, pampered. She just stared at us through the twigs and branches.

I gave up, went upstairs and took a shower. He brought Dandy in, pressing her gently to his chest with one hand. Then he cleaned up the mess and changed the sheets. I wouldn't go now, I said. He told me to stay home. In the midst of the shrieking and obscenities and insults, I felt like laughing, but my pride kept me silent.

Inside the airport, in the Red Carpet Room, all was smooth, now. There was the plush and deep modern furniture in plums and cinnamons and grays. I looked out onto an endless sea of gray and beige and navy suits with vests, businessmen in Brooks Brothers. I was dressed up in a dark silk blouse, china bead necklace, and an elegant wool skirt. Every once in a while, a woman in jeans or an unstylish casual business suit entered.

Ready to embark at the gate, we were an island unto ourselves. Bunched carefully beside his cordovan loafers were his suit bag; a gray canvas Land's End monogrammed briefcase; and his large, rectangular NFL satchel, full and mysteriously lumpy, and on one end a refined-looking badge with his name and number in careful bright blue and red script. Maybe I was just self-conscious with this naked pleasure, I couldn't be sure, but rows and rows of seated passengers about to board with us stared brightly, unblinkingly, about to break out smiling.

Just getting into the plane and settling in, he knew people here and there, a former business associate, and another official, a line judge on the way to Monterrey, both warm and friendly.

I liked the other official. His conversation was witty, quick, intelligent. He had a reddish complexion, was of medium height, stocky, thick as steel, and obviously tough from a lifetime of street knowledge. They were both in the middle section, their seats directly in back of ours. The three of them stood in-between the rows and talked eagerly with a friendly, heightened purpose.

My reserve melted. I felt bold, bantering with the friendly official, responding to his openness. I changed places so that the two officials could carry on with their enthusiasm. I gladly read a book and ate while the two officials shared lunch. I drank wine and was lulled by the hum of the airplane.

There was the strong hint that others whom he did not know nevertheless knew him, evidenced by scattered laughter and tittering, a heartiness heightened by liquor, emanating all around and from the rows behind us. Along with the descent of the plane, the suppressed excitement broke loose as young and middle-aged men cajoled the officials from across the aisle, and the line judge joked quickly and brilliantly with them.

"Boy, you people do an incredible job," a young man blurted joyfully. "It's so *tough*. You've got real guts to take all the abuse. *I* couldn't do it!"

With subdued friendliness, he, the alternate Referee said, "Thanks. We need all the appreciation we can get."

Hurrying inside the hub of the San Francisco airport, we fought again. He could not bear my dragging along, and I refused to allow his impatience. In front of the walking sidewalk, I threw my heavy, shoulder-strap makeup case down in disgust, then picked it up again and proceeded to walk on it at my own pace. Once outside, upon reaching the curb, we waited for a taxi and immediately felt the cold San Francisco weather.

We had dinner in the hotel coffee shop with Bill and Jan, from Cedar Rapids, Iowa. Bill was going to be on the field as the side judge. Jan and I embraced warmly. He and Bill had come through the ranks together the past twenty years and had worked the '72 Rose Bowl. Bill was one of his best friends. Gradually all the officials and their wives surrounded our table with happy noise, and some sat down and joined us.

Suddenly the Referee was standing above us with his hand down on someone's shoulder, smiling quietly. He was slightly sunburned, was neat and conservatively dressed, in a soft blue suede jacket and a white knit shirt. Right away, he gave off a gentle protective kind of power, an anticipation that everything would be all right.

Everyone seemed to know him and his wife, who was now right by his side, smiling greatly. Her lovely face showed through in spite of heavy makeup; her eyes were gray and bright, sparkling joyously, with circles of frosted white around them, playing up the smiling lines. She was truly pretty, a gracious lady. I felt a tug as I looked at them with longing.

"Hi, Ace," the Referee said to his alternate.

I was at breakfast at 7 A.M. the next morning with other officials and their wives. Looking through the large window at the opaque grayness beyond stimulated a hypnotic hazy fog behind my eyes, the early morning in a new and different place, all the food (too much), and I was stuffed, delightfully so, like a sleepy child. The aura was loud and gregarious. Here began hard hilarious laughing among the wives. I and another wife were the butt of jokes because we always ate too much.

A friend planned to take three of us sightseeing while other officials would be doing leisure things and J. opted to stay in the hotel, greeting those arriving, and taking care of business. There was to be a dinner for three thousand guests that night. The officials weren't going, just the wives. John Denver would be there! And the Pointer Sisters. Ten times he urged me: "Be back at four."

At parting time, I was reluctant to leave. I touched his arm and looked up at him brightly and I could feel a light perspiration under his sweater.

The friend had planned an immaculate itinerary. He took us to the highest hill, and stopped the car so we could grasp a breathtaking view of the city.

He said, proudly, "This I call the "First Impression Point.'"

Carelessly, I touched the handle and the door flew open and I fell out, and the suddenness of it and the fear of almost rolling down the hill made us laugh hilariously.

It was cold. Fisherman's Wharf. A mug from the Left-Handed Shop (I am left-handed.). Ghirardelli Square. Spontaneous acts on the streets; one, at the cable car stop, a juggler of bowling balls, machetes and flaming rods all at once. A cold ride around the Bay, to Alcatraz, with hot chocolate that wouldn't dissolve, a plain doughnut, coffee.

Back at twenty to five.

"John is so professional, so good, so organized," he said. "He's been with the league for twenty years."

"That's good. He deserves to do what he's doing, to be the Referee. You're lucky to have him."

That night, all the wives, all dressed up, climbed onto a van to be driven to a sumptuous hotel. Lined up along the curb, all the husbands sent us off, like gentlemen, howling jokes, smiling, smiling almost too much. They were all so handsome, so manly.

It was all mixed up. No one met us at the first stop, like they were supposed to. After a long time of searching and waiting, someone advised us: "Take one of those funny cable cars."

We piled on. Everyone on the car was going to the party, all giggling and laughing. I sat in the open part, facing the kaleidoscope of the city. I made room for a skinny exuberant young man from Dallas, starting out in computers, and our ongoing conversation was lively for the entire ride to the hotel.

Mimes in front of the entrance. The San Francisco Strings in formal dress serenading on the escalator landings going down. In a progressive line toward the grand doors, rum and chocolate served on silver trays by local beauty queens in sequined dresses. Inside, along the vast walls, giant murals. Actors serving grandiose food: Chinese, Japanese, Jewish, Italian. Seafood. Sweets by Ghirardelli. Ethnic acts on high stages between a hundred tables. All the wives at one huge table sharing the same thoughts about the children in Ethiopia who are starving. Someone said Danny Thomas would be there.

A man stalked me as I whisked across the room and I turned to face him.

"David Stone." He waited, smiling. Oh, it was the little brother of a high school friend, now a middle-aged man. Had it been thirty years? Yes. I embraced him tightly, clung to him. With his wife and son, we ended up talking the night away.

No celebrity showed up.

Back up at the room, the key didn't work. I could hear J. get up slowly to let me in. He had been sleeping since nine.

Saturday. There might be a quiet dinner with the supervisor of officials at a good Italian restaurant. After breakfast there were telephone calls back and forth to our cousin who was also visiting San Francisco.

It was another sightseer day. The van kept winding precariously, so close, so close, along the edges of the soaring cliffs that held us aloft as though to keep us just under the clouds and sky.

The thick, giant, boisterous shafts of sun pouring down between the spaces of the redwood trees in Muir Woods caught us up so that we were breathless, flying, and Wanda from Georgia danced among the mist, the heels of her dainty shoes clicking in clockwork-like rhythm to a military song. We clustered inside a shaft so that it hugged us.

Jan said, softly, “You can feel God here.”

Sausalito. Stopping at the end of the Golden Gate Bridge, looking out over the ocean from high up, we saw little dots that disappeared under the water and then came back up in a kind of syncopation, over and over and over.

Jan: “What *is* that? Seals? Gulls? Ducks?”

Hilarity rose and dipped along with the rising and immersion of the ocean’s waves. Getting higher and higher, we looked far down over the vast sweep of green to seek out the images of Cubist houses clinging to magnificent hills and mountains. It was all Cézanne.

There was the sense of getting along so well, liking each other very much. The wives are from all over: Iowa, the South, Colorado, Florida. We were so comfortable together, laughing all the way. I was teaching Jackie from Key West my half-baked Yiddish expressions.

Looking out over the cliffs felt so good--finally--about what he does. I kept thinking of my father urging me long ago to support and understand him.

"There are blue jackets for the alternates to work the walkie-talkie," Jackie said.

Johnniebelle, from Tennessee: "Do you notice it's MOTHER Nature?"

"We're the strength," I added.

"Hear! Hear!" they all cheered.

The Referee's wife turned to her daughter beside her and suddenly said,

"Did you notice how you called me in a Southern accent?" and, "Did you notice how you called me, 'Joan' instead of 'Mother' this morning?"

I liked her, her sweetness, her elegance, her lovely smile, the lines around her bright eyes.

In the gift shop, we were deflated by the show of endless shelves of shiny caramel-colored ornaments, the skins of animals, raped from Nature's Beauty. In line, behind a dark, handsome couple who were traipsing across California, I saw Hebrew letters on the man's backpack. I pointed and pantomimed to my student of Yiddish:

"What language are they speaking?"

Once more, we giggled.

In the van, going back down and looking out over the now-familiar cliffs, we were sweetly tired, tranquil.

Jan said, "They wait for the season to end, and for it to begin again."

Hurt and pouting, I said, "He was always traveling."

Jackie: "We all waited for them to come home."

"But he traveled in his regular job, too; I was always waiting for him to come home," I protested, wanting empathy.

Pointing at me gently, Joan offered,

"She *really* had to wait."

Jan: "They travel, we like to be alone. It passes."

I pressed on: "Now that his weekly travelling has stopped, I've had to adjust to his being home. Unexpectedly, I hear his voice and there he is, behind me or in front of me."

Gazing through the windows, they all nodded and for a time were silent. Almost back at the hotel, we suddenly decided with capricious glee that somehow we could do the impossible: We were going to get to China, Israel, Russia, Europe--together.

Back in the room, his brown eyes flashed upon seeing me enter, dragging gifts I had bought from a stopover at the Hyatt Hotel, and this grew into an argument over time, being ready.

"You'll never get the heavy mugs into--. How are you going to carry those glass mugs--?" Frustrated, he let his words drift off. Then, almost as an afterthought: "You *know* I'm nervous."

The cousins had come in a tight group to see him. He couldn't get out of his meeting, so they went away. We called them with regrets that we could not be with them later because there was an important dinner, which segued into his repeating the time for dinner, and further, that the next morning I needed to be ready at ten forty-five to go to the game with the wives and the officials and that there would be a police escort.

"Be on time," he told me over and over, his voice more and more taut. I told him to stop:

"You told me, once, twice."

Incredibly, the argument heightened, and in-between our back-and-forth accusations, he dashed in and out, flicking his wrist. Abruptly, he picked up the postcards I had bought, saying he was going to mail them, then whipped the door open and it slashed the air; to my surprise, it only closed with a whooshing sound. I felt like crying.

When he came back, I saw that he was happy, with a subdued excitement that was so familiar to me in his boyish quivering of deep breaths. I was so relieved and so touched.

"Wanda bought gloves for you for the game. They wouldn't let me pay. Isn't that thoughtful of them?"

I thought of all the people who had come in and out of our life, and hoped that these would not disappear.

We paused in front of the mirror above the sink just as I finished dressing. He looked deeply at me.

"You're so glamorous, I don't even know you anymore--. You have a whole life that I don't know about."

We were driven to the Italian restaurant in special vans waiting for us. It was quiet, low-key. Some wine, none for the officials. Pins were passed out to wear for identification the next day. The officials slowly clustered on one side of the room, their laughter wholesome and jubilant. From out of nowhere, drunken fans suddenly broke into the room, and in loud, slurred voices, declared that Miami was going to win. One of them stood out from the rest, an orange cap sloppy over his forehead. It was suddenly quiet, the officials abruptly serious.

"Funny, funny," J. murmured, sarcastically, resenting the blot, having known the ugliness before.

During dessert there was bubbling curiosity by the wives.

Jackie said, "What flavor ice cream is this?"

I said, quickly, "Watermelon."

Jackie: "But don't you think it's too *sweet*?"

I rushed back: "With peppermint!"

In the California-San Francisco cold we ran in little shivering steps back to the van, the lingering vapor whipping from our mouths, which instinctively made our lips stay open. Child-like, Jackie rushed up from behind us, declaring excitedly,

"It's champagne-sherbet!"

Back at the hotel, near the young, bleary-eyed salesman selling tee shirts and souvenirs at a long table, the two alternates, and we, their wives, lingered, chatting, eagerly wanting to share something, not wanting to go to sleep. Wanda's and Bob's voices were thick and soothing, blending into one incredible Southern accent.

'I'll never forget Wanda's bright, dark, forever-smiling eyes. I'll never forget her smile,' I thought to myself.

Sunday:

The morning of the game we awakened early; there was good feeling between us. We leisurely discussed the too-much clothes issue.

"I was worried about bringing just enough for each event, but I brought *too* much: two extra jeans outfits and a dressy outfit."

"I did, too. I brought two extra pairs of slacks and a sport jacket that I'll never wear."

"Never--ever--?" I teased.

We laughed a little. He was happy, calm:

"I'm not nervous. If there's a controversial call I'm to take off my blue jacket, run out onto the field and investigate."

A pause.

"John said to me, 'We have confidence that you'll make sure everything goes well; we could have chosen a Referee who rated *tenth*, but we wanted *you*! YOU!' "

He laughed slightly, really pleased. He went down to the lobby, and after a time called me on the room telephone.

"Hi--!"

I imagined his face right then: buoyant, expectant, the essence of his boyish personality. I knew then how much he loves me. He came back up to get me and we went down to the coffee shop holding hands.

There was again hilarity among us, the three wives. Tom, the umpire, rose from the next table, looked over at us and kidded me about how I was eating. Vivaciously, I offered that we have laughed a lot, how silly we've been, that my stomach hurts from all the insistent laughing.

Wanda tilted her head, smiled, and said,

"But isn't it *good* to be a child again?"

Jackie: "Do you notice how when we're together we laugh; when we're with others, there's total silence?"

Wanda: "My throat is sore from hysteria!"

We were in a van at the head of the procession, escorted by a policeman on a motorcycle on either side, while the officials were in another one behind us. All along the way, people inside cars that passed by looked through their windows at us, straining to catch glimpses of who we were. I sat up, unexpectedly thrilled by the attention. A red compact car cut off our driver. Calmly, without hesitation, the policeman veered over, making strong hand signals, and the offender disappeared.

For three miles after getting off the freeway, the boulevards had been emptied just for us. Crowds were lined along the curb on either side, one long procession watching, waving. Every once in a while someone boldly jutted out, holding a sign overhead that read, "Tickets to the Game."

"If my mother could only see me now!" I hollered.

Encouraged by their delight, I shifted to the left and to the right, and with one hand, making the sign of the cross, blessed the crowd.

At the stadium, the van stopped smoothly and confidently inside an area set aside for it to park, with a large, eager crowd already waiting, held back by yellow tape. Their eyes were collectively sparkling, adoring.

"We better put on our dignified airs--!" someone taunted.

The stadium staff clustered at the door as it opened, greeting us with welcoming smiles. They helped us down the small steps, each offering a hand, one at a time, as we alighted like royalty, automatically averting our eyes like celebrities do, smiling vacuously. Cameras clicked incessantly. I felt like giggling, as this was the most fun of all.

Out of the van behind us, the officials got out, looking like the gentlemen they are, neat and well-groomed and carrying their heavy satchels importantly. The stadium staff wandered over to them as they alighted, confronting them with logistics, mingling between us. In the middle of it all, the officials came to us and gently kissed us good-bye, and, once more, I was reluctant to leave him.

No one told us how to get to an extravagant pre-game buffet lunch for the press and the stadium official couldn't help us, but we ultimately found it. Johnnie-belle's son and daughter came in, shivering, more than an hour late, because they had been waiting for the bus at the wrong place. We all took over and soothed them, while their mother remained distracted about their circumstances. The entire feast was lined along the wall up front: fish, meat, chicken, rolls, sweets, wine.

We searched for the right gate while the passionate crowds swelled all along the wall of the stadium, circling it, until there were two tributaries of humanity going in opposite directions, passing one another, then rising like waves in the ocean, melding into one mass, enveloping us, so that we were then bumped into and forced along the outer rim where bicycles were being walked and limousines were parked and waiting. Confused and lost, we pressed on, as though through a sludge of peanut butter, trapped, stopped. We all smelled panic. Will we ever get out?

We found our seats in the large press area, just under the press box. We were delighted when we discovered a gift at each seat, a classy tote bag with a collection of prizes: a seat cushion with a bright rainbow logo; a navy canvas lunch box with the Super Bowl logo on top, and inside it, a sandwich with two different halves (turkey and ham), a bottle of grape soda pop, an apple, a banana, a bag of potato chips, a bar of Ghirardelli chocolate, a set of white plastic dinnerware wrapped in a white paper napkin with a gift-box ribbon curling around it. Underneath each seat, there was a green clipboard with a football field design, and a marking pen.

We sat in a line on the bench, close together, tight, blankets and purses and food overlapping, standing and sitting to let others in, holding everything against our bodies. Johnniebelle came an hour late due to the mass of crowd, she said, regretting that she missed the kickoff. She struggled to put film in her off-brand camera, and I and the man on the other side tried to help her, but we couldn't figure out how to do it, either. Then, her purse and the extra jacket she brought along slipped out of her grasp, and I put the purse inside my own, making a little more room. The men in front of us were drinking and standing up for too long and too often, holding onto everything in their possessions, but it all slid down, anyhow.

Jackie pointed him out first. She and I watched him on the sideline. He was wearing earphones and a blue jacket over his uniform; his strong back was facing us, and we could not see his number underneath. He looked young, virile, athletic. His calves, in the black stockings, emphasized his tight muscles. For a moment, he looked around, searching. All during the game, we could hear messages sent to the press box, and then the announcer repeating them aloud.

The half-time extravaganza, the field, a huge stage. BRILLIANT COLORFUL JOYOUS Too much to look at at once, everywhere, all over the field. Costumed dancers on high, giant, painted stages. Bands with colorful bandleaders, their arms hyper, emoting. Strong, joyous voices orating grandly. Dancers hyped. Huge sparklers all around, framing the field. OOOOHHHH The enormous crowd sighed in unison, as one.

After each quarter, photocopied statistics were passed out by a young man waiting in the aisle for the extras.

"Save them for him," Jackie said, but I didn't.

We entered the big after-game dinner, after being checked in by a young staff in blazers who looked meaningfully at the pins we wore, and we felt important. The officials and their wives were sitting all around a huge round table and glowing across at one another (He said, happily, that he would have liked the stats!). For a long time I had thought about what I would say to him on this, the final night after the game.

"I've never been as proud of you as I am right now," I murmured evenly, as his eyes, now gentle and again boyish, were deeply attentive upon my own, showing that he loves me, so much so that he often aches. He leaned to me, and we kissed.

"Hey-y--," the Referee buoyantly admonished us from across the table, and tipped the champagne goblet (engraved, "Super Bowl XIX") toward us a little bit.

"It's something in the water," I joked, feeling very shy.

Then, they all kissed! The officials laughed a lot, exhausted after working so hard, sharing the joy of a beautiful accomplishment, as the wives watched them, their eyes intoxicated. I thought that just months ago, I would have felt strangely sad and would have wept silently inside in the midst of all the happy noise. But, no, tonight, I was happy, too. John, the Referee, came over, hugged me, sweating and very happy, then said, affectionately to him: "Ya' bum!"

He walked us out as we left.

Outdoors, I saw the friendly young man from Dallas whom I had met on the cable car, dallying at the entrance. I was delighted that in a big city one can again meet someone newly familiar in the midst of a huge friendly party where people are glad to see one another.

Right away, he said, "I'm dying to get into the party to see some Dallas players."

Back inside, I scurried about, searching for the Referee. He was taken up by the mood of my idea and the euphoria of the evening, and he, too, scurried about, and quickly secured a pass to the party for the fan of the Dallas players, so delighted by his special triumph.

The next day, Monday, on the flight home, the friendly blonde stewardess gave us tips on our next trip to San Francisco. Still feeling the aura of the sharp, witty jokes and ideas that bounced off me and Jackie, I wrote her a letter.

He said, "John's wife is so nice."

Then, "Pete Axhelm was at the party. He kidded me about his article on me."

We ate too much for breakfast and lunch. We had a stopover at the Salt Lake City airport, and I was drawn to the gift shop filled with handmade Native American artistry. I bought tiny and delicate pierced earrings made of turquoise and silver teardrops and dramatic sterling silver drop earrings with curlicue posts that will hang below my earlobes.

We switched planes.

"Frank Gifford came in and talked to me."

I looked up from the letter, distracted, and gazed at him in acknowledgement, but I was really absorbed with the certainty that I had probably gained seven pounds.

"The San Francisco players all talked to me, said, 'Hello.' I didn't even think they knew me."

An image flashed of the young man in the parking lot who idolized him after he did the Rose Bowl. He stood securely, in a trench coat, hands in his pockets, legs slightly apart, facing him, eyes brightly and deeply glowing, beaming a devoted smile in steadfast adoration.

"I've always wanted to meet you, to shake your hand," he had said.

The hand had come out eagerly and carefully. The handshake between them was strong, secure and lasted for many seconds. I saw the reaction, the reward in his face, the deep satisfaction, the concentration on things unknown to me.

In the limousine ride home from the airport, he reflected,

"Think my car will start?" It had been a record twenty-seven degrees below zero while we were gone.

A pause. He tilted his head at me, his face having that concentrating look.

"We'll plan that trip. We're going to live a little," he said matter-of-factly, almost sternly.

A couple of months before, he had driven his mother to the dentist. He felt good about helping her, doing something for her. His parents had gotten older, and he had begun to panic about that, but had come to accept it. He was even calm about it.

In the car coming home, in the silence, his mother had turned her face to him.

"You've become a fine man," his mother said.

Aldo Moro

That first morning at five-thirty at the Campino Airport, the airplane came to a heavy stop. I turned back for a final look at it; it was still as a silver bird. We stumbled through the loose peeling doors that opened to the terminal where officials would be waiting to welcome us. There was an overwhelming discomfort at being displaced. To add to it, we were confronted by men in trench coats and dark berets who were pacing and chattering while flinging their hands at one another. One or two of them would come toward our group and expectation would rise, but they kept on chattering and ignoring us and our hopes would sink. Someone found out that they were frustrated because we had come to Rome much earlier than expected: The pilot had done his job too well.

A sudden mild applause erupted behind us and I turned around to find the source. Dressed in their uniforms, our crew members were now graciously forging through our crowd to go outside; and, in spite of bewilderment and restlessness, the passengers were warmly showing their appreciation for delivering a safe journey. The stewardesses came first, pale and tired but smiling in unison, their little beige capelets slightly rumpled and dull in the early morning. The weary pilots followed, but their eyes were bright and friendly.

A woman guide appeared, motioning for us to follow her to the bus that would take us to our hotel and then she spread her arms open wide as we filed in line beside her.

I watched her from my seat on the bus as she faced us all the way down from the head of the aisle.

"Si, seeynora-a-ah--," in a deep voice in answer to a question, her face direct and forward to the person, with certainty and confidence. Interrupting an apology for incessant curiosity: "Look, seenyorra--: I am here for jus' that. (the final t, pronounced, "d").

"To ask questions is to find out, to get answers, to know. Be glad to ask me anyeetheeng you weesh. You must be forceful and ask, or I cannot do my job and help you. Please--." (with firmness) "Ask anytheeng, everytheeng--!"

Her full, true-red lips rounded words clearly and her fingers fanned and fluttered. Her black eyes meandered and lingered longingly through the glass to stress a point, hinting at the depth of history waiting to be discovered with her guidance in the enormous hills beyond. I was entranced by the mixture of firmness and delicacy that was her persona: long tapered nails, deeply red and shiny as her lips; a full round face with skin like milk; hair curly and below her ears, a deep shiny black that I had never seen before. Her gestures encouraged us to follow her gaze and, though exhausted, we watched as the bus took us through a poor, hilly area that was heavily populated.

Right away, we reveled in the sightseeing of Rome. Several of us became a little family, sharing a mild euphoria as the spring weather enhanced our awe of the towering ancient wonders surrounding us. We plunged into the crowds that are everywhere, tramping on and on so that our soles and heels were numb. We came to expect the daily tourists' weariness in the feet and head as a kind of reward for our efforts.

"Save me a seat on the bus. I'll meet you down in front," we would say after the continental breakfast the hotel had prepared in its intimate modern dining room, a very light first meal of the day of brioche and cappuccino. What a difference from some hearty American breakfasts of omelets and pancakes with maple syrup!

All Rome was clean. Shopkeepers swept the curbs with old-fashioned brooms that reminded me of witches in fairy tales. Every day, at six in the morning and five in the evening, older ladies with gray hair and buns in back, wearing clumsy clogs and long drab housedresses, came to familiar spots and onto the cobblestones carefully set bowls of water and food for the dogs and cats that run freely, unobtrusive, unharmed.

The Coliseum was wrapped grandly around a huge corner, the sun flat on its ancient bricks, its history blazing. I was stunned by the sight of Italian women on the corner closer to us in casual groups chattering loudly at one another, flashing their hands, ignoring the astonishing wonder behind them. All were copies of one another, short and very thin, with light delicate faces and short black hair with strands dyed a feeble red.

All Italian men everywhere were slim and well dressed in smooth shirts and sports jackets and sleek pants. Even tour guides and cab drivers wore ties.

In the dark corridors of sophisticated shopping areas, slender, smartly dressed women were often arm-in-arm in twos, shaded by the wide and ancient caramel-colored buildings that towered over them. In wrinkled leather boots and dark skirts and dresses and raincoats, they would stop to face one another, talking rapidly and earnestly, their hands flying.

Each day, the fast, clipped tones of their language all around increased until it all came together and sounded like one voice: full, rich, the volume rising warmly at exactly the middle of an idea, rolling downward dramatically, then concluding with curiosity and patience, expecting an answer. Always, there was the necessity of physical accenting: heads forward slightly to the other person in earnest; hands up, with fingers spread; or hands closed with fingertips touching the thumb. Over all, I imagined that they were sounding out the most romantic or most worthy declarations that would change the quality of the world.

Every day brought new discoveries. On the first morning, we stepped gingerly down the little steps of the hotel onto the unfamiliarly narrow sidewalk. The air was unexpectedly light and refreshing, encouraging us to brave the strangeness all around.

We were captivated by the plazas and their wide cobbled boulevards, where armies of Fiat 500 automobiles sped continuously as one, like rivers, without stopping, toy cars moving by themselves, so tiny that the passengers were invisible from where we stood to watch them. A Volkswagon Beetle showed up speeding among them and we laughed heartily at the giant oddity it suddenly appeared to be.

We saw Fiats parked in bunches next to curbs and in the middle of traffic. Here and there one would be set onto a narrow sidewalk right in front of a shop or store because when it died, it was just too insignificant to repair and so small that it wouldn't get in anyone's way, so it was left there.

On our first day of sightseeing, we crawled into a taxicab to take us back to our hotel after we visited the Borghese Gardens, four of us folding our bodies inside it, to make room for one another! On another day, late in the afternoon, I turned around irresistibly to watch a small, square automobile in bright yellow swerve smoothly around the empty Piazza de Popolo.

Roberto became our favorite tour guide. We invited him to our room one evening to share champagne with us before dinner. He was friendly and ever smiling, with straight black hair that came to a slight wave over his forehead. His round face was flushed and boyish and his teeth incredibly straight and white. He seemed American in his eagerness to be friends and show us the way.

While we were standing in single file in the aisle of the stilled bus in front of the Plaza Navonna, ready to depart, Roberto, standing in front, raised his palm in a declaratory gesture to halt us, his chin up to reach through to the last person. He directed us that the way we were trying to cross the streets just would not do. He had been watching our nervous attempts to reach any point of interest, wobbling with uncertainty on the edges of the curbs, searching with no luck for a way to slice through the eternal traffic that never stopped politely to wait for us. There was only one way to go, he advised: Once we had sighted the destination across the piazza we had to move with (1) determination, and (2) speed.

"There is an unspoken, unwritten law among drivers," he told us. "They have an agreement not to kill pedestrians, especially American tourists!"

From that moment on, we floated over the thick piazzas filled with a relief we did not really trust, and a self-imposed daring.

MORTE AL FASCISIMO.

NO AL FASCISIMO.

Red and black, tall, jolting letters and symbols burned onto the bridge that rose like a hill over the Tiber River that divides Rome.

Swastikas. Nazi symbols, everywhere. I was horrified by the openness of it all.

Everywhere: MORTE AL FASCISMO.

Strident adult letters imitating the rebelliousness of children's erratic handwriting. The letters glared monstrously, smearing and gouging exquisite pedestals that exalted ancient Roman bodies richly veined while in silent motion. The overgrown marble monuments were elaborate, timeless, ever reaching, rising still, preserved forever in their original beauty, always surrounding the people; the words, modern epithets burned like gas into the monuments, lowered their dignity so much so that the marble bore the look of dull, raw plaster.

Roberto and the other guides pointed to this basilica, that obelisk, the Palace of Justice, and the piazza monument, and nothing was mentioned about the politically red scrawls, the black symbols, the black letters. I forced myself to settle in to looking past them, pretending that they were not important, maybe not there at all, that the venerable panorama of statuaries was eternally unaltered.

Ahhhh, the rich canopies of trees in rows; the narrow cobblestoned streets; the huge, wide palaces converted to modern stores; the old and narrow tall hotels with their thick black doors slightly ajar, pointing inside to their dark lobbies with marble floors. Outside, enormous vases and jugs against the sides of marble buildings. A glimpse through the leafy pattern of black wrought iron portals revealed a city garden in front of a stone house. Dark alleyways. The hams hanging pale and beige on ropes in small dark windowless groceries that were flush on the narrow sidewalks.

And then, again, there they were, undeniably red, erratically scrawled on caramel-colored palaces:

MORTE AL FASCISMO!

The weather should have foretold the tale: chilly, gray, overcast. For the first six days, Rome had been mild and sunny, ranging in the sixties to seventies. It was Thursday. We set out in high spirits. In spite of the dull weather we looked forward to seeing Florence, that city of all cities of art and culture.

I sat in the middle of the bus, collecting my thoughts and reliving sensations of the trip so far. The sides of the bus were solid glass, with nothing to bar the tourists' vision. Here in the very beginning of spring, hills were bursting with verdant lush green between wide natural grassed steps that climbed effortlessly to the sky.

And it was all clean, everywhere. There were farms spread wide, with olive trees black and twisting, set in rows, held in place with ropes at angles sprouting from the black earth to their trunks. There were yellow carpets of corn that had been pulled and left to grow wild. Here and there would be a small house of stucco with wooden doors and window shutters. It was impossible to do anything but watch through the wide expanse of window. All on the bus were quiet or sleeping on this early morning.

And the guide's manner was infectious. From her seat in front she spoke quietly into a microphone that she held close to her lips. She told little stories to keep us amused. Her voice hummed with a flip of Italian depth, as the microphone increased its softness and it covered the length of the aisle like a soothing carpet.

Watching the side of her face every now and then as she turned sideways made me think of other Italians who had made an impression. She was tall and full-figured with very black thin hair that came to the back of her neck.

The mellow hum of the language floated through my head as we rode to Florence. Then it became the chatter of the language flying through me as we kept on, the hills and houses fluttering past in a darkened, shimmering pirouette. Everything I saw was like one enormous tulle ballet skirt brushing against the window, the barest, lightest light on the layered edges. I was sleepy, but roused myself every now and then, for I did not want to miss the countryside.

The somnolence so typical of travel pervaded. The sets of plush dark seats and the backs of peoples' heads marching to the front on either side of the darkened aisle drew my lazy attention. And then I felt mischievous. Perhaps I could tickle someone's neck, hair, etc.

Suddenly a man's magnified voice floated above as though a radio had been turned on and the dial manipulated to make the words abnormally loud and clear. Two rows or so up a man twisted around in willing discomfort, his neck ringed in concentric circles, to face us with a general informative look, seeing no one in particular. His mouth was partly distorted as he spoke.

"Someone was kidnapped---."

His face darted back to the front for an instant and then back again to us. His finger pointed high over the sea of heads to the front: "--the radio--." Non-committal, pleasantly indifferent, he twisted back again, then jogged softly in place, and settled back in his seat.

I wondered mildly who the kidnapped person might be. An innocent citizen, a man, I imagined, walking casually and pleasantly in short light shirtsleeves down the street, hands in pockets, with no general purpose in mind, suddenly whisked away for ransom. I had read about the multitude of kidnappings of relatively average people in Rome. Professional people, true, but more or less ordinary because they were not statesmen, or famous, but working on a day-to-day basis along with the multitude.

Knowing this before we came had made me fearful. I had conjured up an expansive wildness and darkness and dirtiness of the city of Rome. I had not wanted to come at all in the first place, afraid of taking a chance, preferring to remain safely at home.

But there were other considerations---did I really deserve to go? And I was afraid to fly. We hadn't taken a trip in a long time, and the winter snow had been historically deep and paralyzing, and--and--. But then, most importantly: Our daughter, who was living in Austria, wanted to be with us.

I remembered that in all the buses of all the tours we had been on, there had been no radio visible and none had been heard. And then this, this sudden voice out of nowhere. I shrugged the thoughts away, and leaned my forehead against the glass, staring out at the countryside once again.

We came to Florence, the bus winding through its damp, dark, snake-thin streets. The day was oddly silent and still stubbornly gray, inside this city that was supposed to be golden, brilliant, colorful, with the sense of ancient art in the air.

The bus came to a heavy stop opposite a large circle in the pavement, made up of long, rose-gray bricks fanning out like a butterfly from its center. There were soldiers bunched together inside it, long rifles slung over their shoulders and falling all the way down their sides; leafy bush-patterned trousers billowing at their ankles above high black boots with buckled flaps, the boots shining impeccably. It was apparent by their restless body language that they were bewildered, lacking direction.

Our guide quickly jumped off the bus without speaking and strode up to the soldiers. After a short time, he skirted back up the steps, stopped next to the driver's seat, cleared his throat and settled his feet apart. There was no need for him to reach for his microphone, as we all were silent and attentive, waiting for his announcement.

"Our prime minister has been kidnapped. The country is searching for the thugs who did this. The military is halting everyone for proof of identification. As tourists, you are all going to have to show your passports."

The growing confusion and terror grew in the air inside our bus. We were strangers in a strange country, and this was so alien to us. We sat, frozen in our seats.

We looked out to see ordinary people pacing, harried, on the outer edge of the center of the piazza. One, his hand over his eyes and forehead, was shielding his horror. Another, his eyes wildly exasperated, hair flying, was just running across the circle.

The soldiers marched heavily up the three front steps of the bus, their weighty rifles still dangling from their shoulders, their bulk and height seeming to touch the ceiling. I suddenly felt guilty for being an American, for living in a country of freedom.

From the aisle, the soldier managed to stand in front of me, up close. As his hand reached for mine, I gave him my passport. The texture of his uniformed trousers filled up my vision so that I could see the fibers. I looked down at his boots that seemed to leap up to me: 'Mussolini,' I thought.

The feeling of being trapped with no way out blanketed us all. I turned my head and stared through the window to witness our male guide now standing outside the circle of soldiers, his hands outward at his sides, pleading. There were murmurs that trickled back to us from the passengers in front, that halfway down the aisle from us, a man had stood up quickly, put his camera in front of his nose, and clicked away to capture the images of the soldiers still standing on the piazza. As a result, the soldiers wanted to take us all to jail and deal with us later; our guide was begging for us to be exonerated right there and then.

Most of us knew that, in Europe, unlike the United States, it was forbidden for photographs to be taken of those in uniform, especially government employees and the military. My heart beat with anger at the self-centered man who had done this to offend our gracious hosts and for him to be apathetic of the fact that he had seriously put us all at risk. 'A dumb, shallow, selfish American,' I thought, for not understanding and respecting the standards of a foreign country.

The guide finally came back to the door and scooted up to the front. Up until now, even while explaining the danger and disaster to us, he had maintained his professionalism by not betraying any emotion. But now, his eyebrows were wrinkled, his eyes weary with worry as he announced that we had been formally released without being penalized, politely omitting the reason or person responsible for his ordeal.

I felt deeply grateful, understanding that the only reason we were let go was due entirely to the empathy of our tour guide, who, with urgency, convinced the soldiers that an American tourist meant no harm, just that he was unaware of the seriousness of his action.

I looked back out the window. Outside, up close to the bus, a young blond man was on tiptoes reaching up to each window, one-by-one, starting with the front and moving back, his skewed pink lips wet and glossy, a horrible smile on his face, slobbering, drooling, making obscene gestures with his fingers up toward each set of passengers, his joy sickening.

Then I remembered the images of Italians who had been consistently staring at us with derision on their faces as we had formed lines to alight and descend from the touring buses.

As the man came closer and closer to my window, my disgust turned to anger, then revenge. I would punish him, give him what he deserved, do what no other tourist on the bus would willfully do. Anticipation made my heart pump fast.

He came to me, and the closeness of him, barred only by the large thin pane of glass, repelled me even more. I looked down at him, my eyes hard, I hoped, my face otherwise expressionless, as he moved his fingers awkwardly and obscenely under my nose. With no emotion showing, I raised my hand and gave him the finger.

His head jerked erratically, he leaped up to me, his blue eyes blazing, his fingers scratching madly at the window each time he tried to smash his fist through the glass.

In the seat next to me, Jerry, my husband, suddenly yelled,

"WHAT ARE YOU DOING????" YOU COULD GET US ARRESTED!!!"

At that instant, the bus pulled away with a heavy groan and we were off to a jewelry store that had invited us to shop; and then, to a monastery where a friar had offered to give us lunch and welcome us to Florence.

Incredibly, another person up front bolted upright out of his seat, his camera already in front of his nose, and began clicking away.

My mother-in-law, sitting near us next to my father-in-law, bolted upright, herself, and, righteously representing all of us, unafraid, yelled,

"Stop it, you idiot!! Don't you understand? You are going to put all of us in jail! SHUT UP AND SIT DOWN!!"

Quietly and slowly, he did just that.

As the bus turned away, we espied a replica of Michelangelo's, "The David," in front of the piazza's museum that contained the real sculpture inside, where we were not allowed to enter on this uniquely horrific day. Our bus parked in front of a jewelry store that sold only gold, and Jerry's mother bought a feminine rope necklace with tiny diamonds interspersed between the delicate knots. Then, off to the monastery, where we ate at a long table in the outdoor atrium, with columns enclosing us in. The brown-robed friar walked on air, his hands crossed behind him as he smiled and circled us, giving us hospitality and sending out his wish that we were enjoying ourselves. I admired his kindness, the quiet sacrifice he made for us, in the midst of the terror surrounding his life.

Two days went by as, trembling, still confused, we visited more icons, our awe and euphoria having left us.

We flew home and after many hours disembarked into our homeland, dizzy, exhausted, our bodies thick with erratic sleep. As usual, it took me a month to recover, perhaps with the added burden of our very unusual journey.

Three months later, American newspapers reported that the Prime Minister of Italy, Aldo Moro, had been discovered at the edge of the ocean's shore, his limp body billeted with bullet holes, having been tossed there by his kidnappers. The articles were sequestered inside, on the third or fourth pages.

As I went about my errands, I looked at other shoppers and, on their faces, I saw unawareness, apathy. After all, there was no need for them to care about kidnapping and kneecapping, so common in a country so far away.

I felt isolated, a single power deeply affected by the earth-shattering tragedy of another peoples, having witnessed its aftermath close up.

Rice Paper

THE CAB BUMPED TO A STOP RIGHT IN FRONT OF THE HOTEL. A SANDY-colored path bordered by elephant leaves tipped in pink curved all the way to the entrance, which was covered by a small awning. A tall palm tree on either side rose amidst little forests of accordion-pleated fronds dripping with curly threads. We felt the newness: The air, even inside the taxi, was close, tropical.

A bellman in a splashy Hawaiian shirt, shorts and sandals spurted from the entrance. We followed him down the path and to the right over a shaded walkway where, overhead, colorful parrots were in a line in round cages hung from the ceiling. We turned to the left, around a corner, to find a pond circled with unfamiliar rocks and native tropical ferns sprouting from the crevices, where white geese were pleasantly swimming, together and apart. Beyond, an enormous bleached patio with aged bamboo chairs and chaise lounges swung around an aqua-colored pool, very long and kidney-shaped. And all above, a sky of soft unwavering solid blue that I had dreamed of but never seen, puffed and powdered with tiny clouds of cotton here and there.

The whiteness of everything--patio, walls, clouds--blared, and the hotness came to its peak when I glared into it, my eyelids boiling and hurting, as was my forehead, and I had to squint, even though a cotton hat was tight around my head, shading my eyes. Aunt Jeanette had warned us that this sun was not like ours back home and we had to be careful. Others told us that it would all be worth it if we were cautious and used the sun lotion #15.

The bellman halted and turned to face us. He was medium height, and muscular, tanned with a reddish tint to it, with curly sun-bleached blond hair. With a small friendly smile, he said that our room would be ready in about an hour and that our luggage was safely stored behind the desk of the concierge by the doorman, whom we noticed, was also dressed casually.

He turned back again and we followed him over the threshold through a wide opening of the hotel as a surge of hot wind followed us. I was compelled to turn back in wonder to grasp the blazing blueness of the sky and ocean, a blue that I had never known. The panorama was a miracle, a painting come alive, colors of it lined up from top to bottom: pure blue sky; potent blue and green ocean; sizzling, yellowish sand; then, deeply green grass, closest to us.

We plunged into bursting yellow light that filled a vast foyer that had captured the exotic outdoors into stillness with its high ceiling and unending, glossy floor, permanently soaked with the sun's rays. Welcoming us was an enormous plant with stalks soaring from a huge deep bowl on top of a round table on a big octagon rug, a pattern of largeness punctuated throughout: feathered fronds reaching for the ceiling, sprouting out of bloated vases; sprawling rugs faded in ancient reds and blues and greens; clusters of sofas and chairs framed in dark tropical woods, scattered all along the whitewashed walls; and glass tables mixed in-between and crowded with covered jars of multiple sizes set on top of them.

We spotted a bright red sofa in a far corner in front of a paned doorway that was closed and seemed to lead nowhere, grateful for its privacy, bouncing with numb ecstasy into its softness, so acutely aware of our tight bones against the cushion.

When it was time, we followed our bellman toward the elevators. Ever smiling, he pushed the door to our room open with a kind of flourish, then stepped back so that we could go in before him.

Just as we swept over the threshold, a masculine voice flowed out of a television set that had already been turned on for us. On the screen, an anchorman in a splashy Hawaiian shirt and black shiny beads was announcing the day's news:

"The police have arrested a suspect for the murder."

What?! Murder- - - in PARADISE??

In the rack next to the concierge's desk the flyer suggested that The Polynesian Village was "a must," because, "seeing the replicas of the villages will impact the general history of The Islands."

We stood in the ticket line under the blazing sun, facing the little hut that was the box office. In back of Jerry, I could feel his glee at being a tourist. He turned to me with a dreamy smile and said softly,

"I love this!"

From the hot spots under the balls of my bare feet inside my gym shoes the fire of dry raw cement crawled between my toes. Here, in line—experiencing that my eyelids were like blinds that would not stay open—I was trying to convince my (blond) self that I was really loving the hot sun.

In the flat canoe made of raw teak, cramped with strangers, we floated on the silken glass water. Our guide created a contagious laziness by the slow movements of his pole plunging to the bottom, then pushing his body forward, spurning the boat to languish, hypnotizing us.

"The waterways were the highways of the ancients," he announced, almost singing a sonorous tune. "The tentacles of the ancient islands reached out to one another so that cultures lived side-by-side. This is how the Polynesian natives of Samoa, Togo, and Fiji traveled in their journeys to one another on rough and dangerous seas."

Covered with mats of wavy leaves, the long table of the luau was spread from end to end with platters of thick juicy pineapple slices; large shining mottled lemons; pomegranates standing with their insides split open, oozing clear purple; and prickly pineapples set upright and crowned with stiff, saw-toothed leaves. There were other moist fruits we had never seen for their purity and fullness.

The lady standing next to me whispered in my ear as we leaned against the table's edge,

"Wait till you visit the Dole Plantation. You have never seen such an abundance of magnificent pineapples in your life, all around you, everywhere you look, as you are just standing there on the luscious red ground they have sprung from, as far as your eye can see."

The mountains were turning black and becoming invisible, so that one had to look into them to make sure they were still there, while the sun bulged over the shelf of the gray horizon against the layers of pale orange, pink and blue, leaving a skirt of magenta under it. Early night flowed in, touching our shoulders, the strangeness of it stirring long ago sadness and regret.

On the outdoor stage, beige boys and men twirled poles of fire, making swift orange and yellow circles against a black background of evening as our eyes glittered and hurt and our hearts bumped. They wore halos of grass across their foreheads, and their bare arm and chest muscles bulged sensuously as they fluttered long knives in dangerous patterns and plunged poles of fire into their mouths, making hot-white ribbons rise from their tongues. There was the rhythmic pounding of their strong bare feet against the wooden stage. Thump. Thump. Thump.

In front of them, beautiful bronze women, with black eyes and splashy red lips and raw, shining black hair that fell to their waists above grass skirts, gyrated to the beats of the drums, their arms in front flowing like the waves of the ocean, their hips beckoning, leis of lavender orchids hiding their breasts, while the men behind them swayed with the heat of masculinity as they hollered fiercely, their smiles daring:

"Hiyah!"

I found myself yearning to be with the silent creatures. I sat at the edge of the pond, and the white geese immediately felt my presence. Even in the water, there was a hierarchy as, in a V, they came to me, their end feathers fluttering. They seemed to be smiling for my sake, their beady eyes riveted at me. One by one, they disbanded, bumping softly against the rim on either side of me.

Later, I walked over to the parrots trapped tightly in individual globed cages in a line hung from hooks under the eaves that bordered a long dark outer hallway that we had seen that first day. They were of pure and solid colors, two in red; two in cobalt blue, and two in yellow; each alone and lonely, not knowing of the others.

I started at the beginning, down the line, facing each up close, my lips tight, then smacking a kiss at one, then another, showing that they were loved, that the world had not forgotten them.

Strolling back to the lobby, I found people scattered leisurely around the pool, smiling and staring in one direction. I turned to see. A hotel employee, with a walking stick by his side, was escorting a goose down the sidewalk back to the hotel. The goose had taken a walk.

On my way up to our room, I looked up to the ceiling with fascination at the squared translucent rice paper fans hung in rows, swaying slowly forward and backward in even rhythm, a contrived touch of Paradise, a modern trace of a primitive way of life, now gone.

The tall, sleek elevator doors bounced heavily and came to rest, then whooshed open.

I stepped in, pushed "32."

The platinum doors began to close smoothly; then, as if startled, the panels trembled and flung apart. Two Japanese men rushed in, and bowed slightly. I nodded.

Up to "12."

The doors opened. Three Japanese women stepped in tentatively, bowed to the men, and smiled. I backed up a bit to make more room.

Next, "15."

The doors opened. Three more Japanese women rushed in. Just after the doors closed, they bowed sweetly, then turned around to face the front, smiling and chattering in low tones. I moved slightly to the rear.

Then, "17."

Two Japanese men entered while in business-like conversation with one another. They instantly stopped to acknowledge the passengers, nodding as they grinned and chuckled. The women giggled softly, bowed in unison, then shifted to get comfortable alongside one another.

I took one large step back, my shoulder blades now flush against the elevator wall. Watching, I was on the outside, looking in, invisible. The consistent chattering had gained a humming, lyrical quality: women smiling, heads nodding, men keeping to themselves.

"20." Ding.

The doors opened. Still chattering, they all got off at once as if they were going to an important meeting together. I sighed, anticipating relief, and stepped forward, grateful for having been given the luxury of the full space of the elevator.

As one entity, outside the doors on stable flooring, the group suddenly stopped short, turned to face me, smiling greatly and sincerely delighted; and with assertive justified pride, they bowed and bowed and bowed. It was as if the elevator doors had paused to accommodate them.

I was stunned! They knew I was there? But I was invisible!! How could they have known of my presence? My heart burst. I wanted to laugh, to shout, to yell with hearty joy!

They stayed facing me, dressed in tourist suits and dresses, as if patiently waiting for me to give some kind of signal so that they could move on.

And then the doors snapped closed.

On the first day, going from the airport to our hotel, our taxi passed The Royal Hawaiian, so pastel and tropical. I thought it the epitome of the historical aura that we had come to experience and right then I longed to stay there to savor its essence. The sun reflected its being, surging pink. At a distance, the symmetry of delicate grayish blue awnings above the tiny windows spread across the façade like eyelashes across the pink porcelain of a maiden's face.

Going to and from our tours, we passed the statue of King Kamehameha I, the sun ever melting over the solid stone replica of him: the strong brown of his skin under the gold of his garments, shown by his arm forward in a proclamation of welcome; the other, holding a royal spear upright; his crown, a helmet shaped like a valiant bird; and a caftan and chest shield protecting his strong legs that were revealed underneath. The paths to our destinations became predictable and then meaningful, as, by seeing him repeatedly, we were forced to understand his essence, his power and his gentleness, that he was a man who would lead his people in their heritage, as one with them.

We stepped tentatively onto the vast wood floor of black sheen in the Iolani Palace, wearing soft pale blue booties over our shoes, automatically handed to us before we entered. There was the sorrowful aura looming of Queen Liliuokalani, large and tall, the last of her reign, the cruelty of her banishment lingering still. I felt her loneliness, her womanly courage.

The pristine floor glowed. Red velvet was everywhere: the wall-to-wall carpet with a pattern of yellow leaves; stiff tufted chairs framed in gold; a round hassock in the center; tall, deeper red window curtains pulled gently open by gold tassels. The throne, set on a platform with small steps leading to it, was draped in the same darker red with a cornice overhead made of large velvet teardrops.

How hidden the truth lies behind this small pageantry! Wrenched from her royal position by British and American businessmen, Queen Liliuokalani chose to avoid the certainty of war, submitting to forceful imprisonment in her own palace.

But she rose above it all, composing songs; writing books and essays; thinking only of her people. She is at once the humble servant and the heroine of her country. She prevailed. Her kind soul lingers.

Back outside, THE Banyan Tree, set in the center of the urban palace grounds, on stage for all to wonder at. Lithe, ancient gray roots flung up! up! to covet the massive torso of the trunk, then higher, higher, to fling over muscular branches that soar like dancers' limbs, then to flow back down toward the soil they were borne from, like slender streams of trickling water, now frozen as they fall.

Pearl Harbor. Ahead, the calm, expansive panorama of rich blue ocean interspersed with folding waves under the pristine, white, sun-drenched Arizona Memorial defies reality. Deep deep down below, in unrelenting blackness, there is the magnified horror of five thousand patriots lying trapped forever, symbolizing their eternal innocence.

The flimsy bridge took us up close, and the stunning reality of history loomed. We saw groups from Japan on a small wooden bridge just like ours, curious, just as we were, to reach the end and alight in front of the entrance. We were shocked to see them pretending to be free of guilt and shame, emulating themselves as simple tourists. How could they be? The Japanese are our eternal enemies.

"What could they be thinking?" Jerry wondered.

Their faces showed no answer. Bland. Dull. Unemotional. I resented them being among us.

"They started World War II," I agreed, bruised from the memory.

"My cousins who came back from the War described their exceptionally brutal torture," I added.

Then I thought of the Japanese tourists bowing to me outside the elevator. I was uneasy: How could I align their polite formalities with the Wartime cruelties of their ancestors?

We jogged in the downtown area, along Kapiolani Boulevard, within crowds getting on buses and throngs standing in front of unadorned department stores. Trotting slower behind Jerry, I became giddy when he plunged between the tiny space between a crunched crowd and the steps of a hot, stuffy bus, not stopping his pace nor adjusting his posture, dancing in place, his head held high like a dedicated athlete.

Back up in our room, I stretched my arms along the balcony railing, where I could see most of Diamond Head on my far left, but not its grand peak that made its image thrilling. The string of tall ivory hotels at the base of it and all along the ocean shore looked familiar, reminding me of Miami Beach. My heart sank because I could foresee that the pure natural beauty of the mountain will be deeply gouged forever by commercial greed.

We went wandering outside around the hotel, searching for the feel of the neighborhood. We came upon a small boutique with its door open in a little stretch of stores. We went inside and asked the young woman behind the counter for directions to the mission houses. She came out and we followed her back outside, where she pointed to the corner where the bus would stop to take us there.

We sat eagerly in the sun on a block of wood. Fifteen minutes passed. We were patient. A half hour later, we allowed that the traffic here was slower than ours back home. An hour passed by, and then the realization hit both of us that we were purposely given the wrong directions.

The driver of the next bus opened the folding door for us to get in. From the curb, we leaned in to ask him how to find the historic mission houses. He said that all we needed to do was to walk five blocks down where the houses would be just over a hill, and they would be recognized by their simplicity and age when they came into view.

We started walking. We came upon a little hill, but no houses. A janitor was sweeping a narrow sidewalk in front of a church with a simple steeple that was settled just in front of the hill. We asked him to direct us to the mission houses. He looked right at us with no change in his face and shrugged his shoulders, told us that he did not know where they were, then looked back down and continued his task.

We decided to keep on, anyway, and give a final push. We strode up the short hill and when we arrived at its small peak we faced the other side. The mission houses were right there, down below! They were small and simple wooden houses, bare and old. The janitor had to know that they were only a short distance away from where we confronted him.

We were white, a minority, and not welcomed. Anywhere. We were the enemy, the rich and powerful Americans. We, now from the mainland, were conquerors, having forced their ancient heritage to blend into our contrary way of living, so different from their own, we who would never honor or endeavor to understand the rich history and culture of the Islands.

And so, paradise has turned out to be everyday life.

The Remarkables

Our trip to Australia and Tahiti was meant to be a reward for company quotas kept and surpassed. We were reluctant to leave, as Jerry's father was suffering physically, having been on the brink of death for the past month, due to bouts of heart failure.

My suggestion--I don't know where this came from or why--was that we go to New Zealand first, then meet the rest of the office people in Australia as planned.

We flew to Los Angeles, then to Hawaii. We decided to visit the outdoor zoo in Honolulu while we passed the time before our next plane took us to Christchurch. There were all kinds of animals that we did not expect to see. There were chickens all over, running and clacking and those sleeping under bushes seemed intoxicated. We had been flying for eight hours and so we were a little disoriented. As we left the path from the zoo, Jerry stood on the corner of the cross boulevards, threw his head back and crowed like a rooster, while passersby smiled and chuckled, as though they understood his frustration.

It was hot in New Zealand. On the way to the hotel, I was terrified while the cab drove on the left side of the roads and all the oncoming vehicles, one after the other, flung at us toward the windshield, destined to smash into us. I gasped and covered my eyes with my hands as the taxi moved fast, without stopping.

The driver murmured, "Oh, this must be very difficult for you."

After a total journey of twenty-two hours, we staggered out of the taxicab into a charming hotel, dragging our thick luggage, then halting in front of the information desk, looking forward to relief from a bellman. The young woman behind the counter smiled weakly, and hesitated.

"Oh, you must not have been aware, but today, all service people went on strike: bellhops, restaurant staff, elevator operators, bus drivers. The entire country is at a standstill."

Our suitcases bounced heavily onto every step as we yanked them behind us up four flights of stairs. We fell into a lovely old-fashioned room with a high four-poster bed and a step stool that led up to it, then threw ourselves on top of the eiderdown comforter, and it was soft, soft, soft, and we sank deeply into it.

The next morning, twenty hours later, we woke up from a heavy sleep. It felt as though we had been napping for only a short time.

We spent that day on a private bus, riding along country roads with cottages and little white wood picket fences hugging them, each one having a tender garden on either side. A tiny grass cemetery with a small number of crude headstones bolted up among several houses. There was a palpable presence of those buried there.

The next day, we took a small plane on to Queenstown. We had made our own arrangements, blindly, I guess, for when we arrived at the "hotel," our taxi driver brought us up over a perpendicular driveway--with his emergency brake on, screeching--and stopped at the peak of it in front of a tiny cone-shaped brick building, with a closet-sized open unlit "lobby" consisting of walls of cement blocks and a folding chair leaning against one side.

This was our chalet, we were told by the un-uniformed man who came out to greet us, and our temporary residence was upstairs, on the singular upper floor. We climbed the cement stairs and entered into a large thinly carpeted room with a floor-to- ceiling stone fireplace that touched the pointed roof on one side and a large bed facing it from across the room and slanted toward a wall of glass facing the famous, magnificent New Zealand mountains.

Being so high up as to *feel* the clouds, our hearts reveled at the vision of the aptly named, Remarkables, glowing purple and blue, with the sun proudly shining down upon them. These titanic formations were the highest we had ever seen, and would change colors, all day long, we were told. To live among them as natives must be heartfelt every day.

One morning, Jerry took the plunge and decided to walk down the formidable driveway to visit the local grocery, sliding and tripping all the way, but he made it. He came back, struggling uphill, cradling glass bottles of milk and orange juice, excited to tell me that he saw a small basket set aside on a counter for any customer to fill it with hand-picked eggs, of any number, not a packaged dozen ready to go.

"This is how it was in America in the 'fifties!" he said, with delight. "You can have as many as you want to take home."

Another day, he saw a ten-year-old girl with a backpack over her shoulder walking--gliding--confidently down the intrepid sidewalk.

"How do you do this without falling all the way down?" he asked her.

"I walk to school this way, every day," she answered, as if that explained it.

We went down to the shore of Lake Wakatipu and signed up for a tour around the mountains. The young woman standing outside the box office of a little wooden house asked if we wanted a snake, the last word emphasized with a sliding, oily tone to it.

"A snake?" we repeated.

"A snake? Do you want a snake?"

We looked dumbly at one another, embarrassed.

"Before lunch?" she went on, urging politely, her pale eyes direct and unmoving.

Together, relieved, we exclaimed: "Oh, a snack! A snack before lunch! Of course! Yes, we want a snack! Thank you!"

The ferry forged ahead like a proud relic from the past, undeterred. Looking out and around at the mountains and enormous airy space circling us, we felt incredibly small and overwhelmed and oddly free.

The mountains were peaked with a blanket of craggy whiteness across the horizon as far as we could see; then slopes of undulating gray and blue and green underneath criss-crossed all the way down, falling behind the deep green and black forest that stood erect over the blue lake dotted white with little waves turning over. Then, as our eyes roved to see more, the file of trees parted, revealing a final slope of pale purple mountain.

The closer we glided to it, the more the darkness of its massive surface spanned our vision, and then the details from far away now loomed: trees and dark hollow craters roaming over bloated snow that curved like white linen sheets thrown askew, and squares of salmon-colored rocks that formed a quilt that billowed, with streams of shadowed folds following in and out of them. There was the solid blue of the contented sky at our backs, and the whiteness of the low, horizontal cloud slicing across the mountain, facing us up close, mocking our longing to see behind it.

We were on a bus inside the mountains. We had been assured that we would be guided by experts, no matter who happened to be our driver. We respected their passion, their earnest desire to make us understand their innate love for the land they had been born into, that the land and they were One.

We bounced along, looking out at the vast bottomless caverns of rock. The guide explained and educated us. The road was cut by hand through the bare cliffs and left raw over a hundred years ago; it took twenty-two years to complete. There are no modern road rails or stop signs or uniformed authorities helping vehicles bypass one another. The speaker kept emphasizing how truly narrow the road is that we were traveling on, that only the most skilled could navigate it, an extraordinary road that demanded the finest skilled concentration.

These are the highest and most beautiful mountains in the world and the most dangerous, he went on. The rumbling urgency in his voice grew with each approach to a sharp turning of powerful rock as the driver aligned the long and bulky bus beside the soaring mountain wall, then inched it around the curve, and, pausing before moving on, in one breathless moment leaving us inches from the cliff edge over an infinitesimal drop. Looking out the windows, drawn irresistibly to danger right in front of us, our subtle fears as tourists mounted.

We came to a twisted opening and a crude sign popped up before us that read,

"THIS NARROW ROAD IS PRONE TO SLIPS."

We went further, the mountain on the left and the cliff edge on the right becoming closer and closer so that at last there was room on the graveled trail for our bus only.

A bus loomed in view and its gigantic tires stopped heavily, the brakes whooshing, its widely sprawling windshield facing us up close, stretching itself across the road.

There was conjecture and commotion as the guide, unperturbed, described what would happen next. We backed up; they backed up. Forward and backward. With awe, we watched as the oncoming driver sidled his bus expertly within an unforeseen width of road; and we, inches away, passed it by, crawling onward, the gravel inside the tire impressions grinding over the ancient soil.

Ahead, the road became so narrow that the mountainside on our left filled the views through the windows.

We came upon another sign of caution:

"ONLY PROFESSIONAL DRIVERS ARE ALLOWED BEYOND THIS SIGN. CARAVANS AND TRAILERS ARE NOT SUITABLE ON THIS ROAD."

We were now so close to the edge on our right that there was only air to look through and when we looked down there was nothing to look at either but air so deep and high and wide, so eternal. Far beyond, tiny in our vision of them, birds soared and dipped, euphoric, because the heavens belong to them.

For the first time ever, I felt trapped by the certainty of death before me. There was no escaping it. My heart froze. How did it come to this, my being here? Why did I permit myself to come? Oh, why didn't I prevent what was now my fate? How reckless of me to want to see the world, not thinking of any possible danger!

Our bus picked up a little speed, and then stopped short to face another sign of caution:

"NO TURN AROUND FOR 6 KM

NO EXIT"

Our tour guide went on in a somnolent, humming tone. Many foolish and overeager people, those not trained to do so, have navigated this road, he declared. As a result, many have fallen to their deaths.

I looked down over the edge as my stomach plunged to my feet and back up again and my heart followed the same route. On the grassy shelf of a cliff lay a crumpled red truck and two cars strewn beside it, one, upside down and rusted, its wheels paralyzed, the other, crushed as if tossed away after being folded into accordion pleats. These were toys that had been mauled by angry children, colors blurred and paled, shapes crushed and impossible to determine.

We spent eleven days in New Zealand, and it was calming, allowing us to savor the essence of immeasurable space surrounding people inherent to their land who wanted no other than the simple life they were born into. It was now time to start the trip the way it had been planned, meeting the office people in Australia, and then going on to Tahiti.

The authorities went out and loaded our luggage onto a small airplane, which sat alone on an open area. Finally, the lady behind the counter, in a moment of absentminded hesitation, informed us that we had a message waiting for us from America.

All was blurred after that. Jerry was speaking on a telephone on the wall of the reception area. The message was from his mother, who said that his father had taken a turn for the worse and was in the hospital. The hope was that he would come home to be with him, with a shadow in her voice that meant his father might not live long enough to see him for the last time.

A speeding up of activity. Annoyed at the receptionist who wasn't smart enough to give us the notification *before* we had our luggage loaded, we went out ourselves to the plane and yanked the bulky suitcases out.

Miraculously, we were able to procure two seats on a plane to Hawaii, which we were grateful for, even though they were not together, but on opposite sides of the craft, across two aisles and three long lines of seats.

Jerry sat next to a doctor who assured him that his father would wait for him. He told a story about a patient of his, who had been dying in a hospital. The doctor told the wife that she should call the two sons right away to say goodbye, as it looked as though their father would not last for more than a day longer.

As the sons entered the room, the father came alive, his eyes suddenly happy and beaming. The three of them played cards around the bed and, to the doctor's astonishment, the father seemed to be well enough to go home and continue on with his life as before. The sons left to go home for the night. During the wee hours, alone, the father passed away.

"Your father will wait for you," the doctor assured him.

It became a dreary, serendipitous ritual. Immediately after each landing, a very nervous and rushed transaction was made for a ticket on the next plane, Jerry explaining that his father was dying. Automatically, the request for a refund was denied, the person behind the counter not looking up from the paperwork.

We went to Los Angeles, then, Colorado. Our last plane ride was, finally, to Chicago. In total, there were four airplane rides, two sunsets, two Thursdays, a total of 24 hours of back and forth culture and time shock. We arrived home on Friday morning, not really certain what day it was.

We went immediately to the hospital, where we dragged ourselves down the hallway as my mother-in-law came from out of nowhere and when close up, spewed her agony onto me,

"Look at you! You look awful!"

I did not trust the doctor, who strode up to us with an unfocussed gaze, as if he were acting, not really caring who we were. He pretended to be frustrated and confused, uncertain as to what to do as a professional, his face and body gestures exaggerated and cold. He expressed to us that whatever he would administer to save my father-in-law would compromise another part of the body. I had never seen a doctor so immature and so insincere.

Jerry's sister had come in from Wisconsin. We all began to pace with nothing to do but wait and worry and feel dread and hope all at the same time. I offered to leave to buy some semblance of dinner that would offer temporary comfort, probably to have something to do to assuage my nervousness.

I dashed out to Poochie's for hot dogs, and when I came back, Jerry and his mother were nowhere to be seen, while his sister stood where I had left them.

"Dad passed away just a few minutes ago."

Dazed, I put the paper bag down on the flimsy table in front of the faded sofa. Jerry came up from behind me and gripped my elbow.

I went into the room where my father-in-law lay, his mouth frozen open from the tube that had been trying to send life back into his body and was now gone. I moved closer.

"I am sorry that we lost our relationship," I whispered. "I loved you from the beginning, when you took me into the family as a daughter."

I felt peaceful. I wanted to say more.

"I know you thought I took your son away from you. It feels selfish and wrong that I feel justified in doing so. I hope you understand."

I came up to the family standing together in the waiting room. My mother-in-law turned and came up to me. Ever stoic, her harsh, light brown eyes were now opaque and wet, her head tilted a bit in a rare flash of visible emotion. She said she was sorry that our vacation had been ruined, that she hoped we would be able to go back someday and make a fresh start.

His mother had said from the beginning that Jerry and I were meant to build a life together, that she would do anything it took for her to reinforce our love for one another.

School

Music

I ANTICIPATED THE TELEPHONE CALL THAT CAME AT SIX-THIRTY IN THE morning. When I arrived to get my schedule, Dena, sitting behind her desk, was readied with her smile of confidence in me, which, I knew, meant that I was a favorite. She gave me every chance possible in many departments other than my own, English, hiring me on a daily basis, and we had become friends. I became gratified for the education that *I* was earning, excited at the privilege of being inside so many different facets of life.

Dena's devoted smile signaled her effervescent willingness to help; she had a knack of mixing business with friendly respect for everyone she dealt with in the arena of the office: clerks, secretaries, the principal, building manager, janitors, department heads, teachers. Unwavering, she sparkled.

She had the personality of a thin, lithe, young woman in her thirties; yet, she was very heavy, and in her 'fifties. Her eyes were small, dark and deeply set close together over a sharply pointed nose. She wore a hairdo that was kind of fancy for the setting in a school building: short, painted a dark burnished red swept high onto the side of her face, set perfectly still as her lively expressions caused her head to be in constant motion. That actually delighted me, as it reflected a mischievous side that made me warm to her.

My assignment, substituting for Mr. Pritchard, who taught film and acting, intrigued me; I anticipated delight in watching students being freely creative, away from the confines of textbooks. It was further enlightening when Mr. Pritchard himself, with a confident, upright posture, very tall and lean, appeared by my side. He said he would show me the proper rooms, get the film and the projector for that day, and familiarize me with procedure before he left. I was relieved to have this real life person-to-person contact, rather than an instruction sheet with obscure writing left for me by a strange teacher whom I would never meet.

His height enhanced the lightness of his walk. He had an easy eager manner, and a vibrant, enthusiastic readiness for the excitement of the day, this day, and any other. He led me upstairs, into and out of various rooms which he travelled in the course of his daily schedule.

"First you go here, leaving the projector; then, you come back for it after the first class."

I laughed, saying, "I can see why you are so thin!"

"Yes!" His laugh exploded lightly. "I'm forever busy."

"Oh," he mentioned hurriedly, at the very last minute, "the acting class knows what to do. They have a project they're working on, so let them take over."

The day went along well, nothing special. The film, as always, proved interesting, a takeoff on Chekov's "The Bet." I read the story, which took about fifteen minutes, and then showed the film.

Mr. Pritchard had said that if I couldn't find the auditorium where the next class was held, the acting class, a student here would show me the way, as he had to be there, too. Instead, he had to do an errand, so he gave me directions on how to get there.

Elaborate they were, but very accurate. Down, down, down, I went from the third floor to the first of this vast school building, built fifty or so odd years ago, and forever dark and heavy with Gothic architecture. When I approached the area I meandered hesitantly for just an instant or two, but found the door exactly where he'd said it would be. It was the entrance to the music room, which I had to wander through first. It was barred by a thick, concrete door. I pulled and it was heavy as it looked.

Once inside, a whole new world, cut off from the one of academia and wild, hyperactive crowds, settled quietly around me. It was a silent, hallowed world where very few were privileged to enter. A narrow corridor guided me; my walk was involuntary. Down the rambling hall I turned and swerved, in and out of sharp corners and sudden turns, passing doors on my right with windows on them. I could see wide rooms and small auditoriums. All held seats for audiences and podiums where students practiced on their violins or sat at pianos or leaned on them. I saw students slithering piccolos and flutes out of soft narrow bags, and a cello standing ready.

A student appeared suddenly in front of me around one of the corners, smiling back at me, meandering with purpose.

"Do you know where you are?" she asked, intuitively.

"Not exactly," I answered, smiling, too. "I'm going to the auditorium, to the acting class."

"Follow me, I'm going there, too," she rejoined, and I did.

We laughed about the strange inconvenience of reaching the theater through the circuits of the music room, straddling over props for plays that appeared here and there. Down the winding, never-ending corridors, and then we stopped abruptly, coming, finally, into an open, dark area with thick curtains hovering over us and hemming us in. Lumber criss-crossed and leaned every which way. As I followed her we circumvented an ambiguous, giant piece of wood, going in back of it to find another curtain framing a long stairway. We walked down the stairway, and lo! an enormous auditorium opened up, and we were finally there.

She slithered down the steps, spilling into the giant room with a tremendously tall ceiling overhead, where the familiarity of her classmates waited. She was lost to me then, as she blended into strange faces, and a strange atmosphere. The students sat in clusters on a large wooden platform below the stage in the center of the auditorium. There were comfortable old chairs placed strategically at two of the platform's corners, and in one a boy sat. All the other students were crowded along the edge.

Over the rim of the large stage itself a young woman sat with her legs crossed, her feet resting onto the platform below it, a large guitar between her knees. She was strumming it aimlessly, humming a tune in a canary's lilting voice, the delicate crystal sounds rising high into the folds of a huge, corniced curtain behind her, lost deliciously within the large sharp shadows above it. Those crowded around her swayed, humming along with her.

They were a happy crowd. I walked to the stage floor and took attendance. There was an air of hesitancy between us when I finished. The students smiled at me pleasantly, expecting nothing and getting ready to do nothing.

I said, "Mr. Pritchard says that you know what to do, that you have a project you're working on."

"Yes," they nodded and mumbled, still pleasantly. They were restless. They didn't begin whatever project they were supposed to be working on. Instead, the girl with the guitar began to sing with renewed effort, strumming with purpose and looking down at her fingers every now and then. Her words were syncopated and laborious, and beautiful, and the students began to resume singing along with her.

I walked to the first row, sat down in one of the plush chairs, and opened Mr. Pritchard's attendance book. I felt self-conscious and wanted to appear busy while deciding what to do.

Some boys got raucous. The one in the chair spilled over backward because the boy sitting at his side by the leg had gotten up and pushed him over. Some of the students became giddy. The boy in the chair laughed loudly, his delight echoing throughout the auditorium, rising up into the high, thick curtain, where it was trapped softly, and died.

I got up, and walked back to them.

"Stop this, please," I said gently, for I didn't want to break their delicious mood. It was infectious.

"If you aren't going to work on your project, we're going to have to do *something.*"

"We just got done with a play," the boy who had overturned explained as he got up, righted the chair and adjusted something imaginary on its arms, "and we're kind of unwinding."

"I see," I said in a half-heartedly officious manner.

"There really isn't much we can do," the boy added, quickly and freely, "because certain materials aren't available."

The girl with the guitar had stopped singing but was strumming randomly again, and humming. A few girls were swaying around her with emphatic movements.

I walked back to my low, cushioned seat, getting a squirming feeling on the top of my skin. What was I to do? Could I use the knowledge from long ago, when I, myself, was an acting student? I'd have to pull up something, quick.

All of a sudden, from nowhere, a tall, gangly boy in a tee shirt and jeans strolled out of the voluminous curtains on my right. He had thick, dark, careless hair. He went across the stage, stopped center, faced the shadowed group and said, his arms hanging limply at his sides,

"Is this a class?"

"Yes!" was the joyous, scattered response. He kept on walking purposely to the left of the stage, into the other wing.

"WAIT!" someone yelled after him, "You can stay!"

He stopped, came back to them a little, and stood.

"Are you sure?" he asked.

"Yes, yes---. Are you a student here?" someone asked.

"No," he said.

"That's okay," a girl hollered gently, "c'mon, and join us."

"What are you doing here?" someone wanted to know.

"Are you looking for someone?" another asked.

"No, I'm just passing through."

There was respectful laughter.

"Actually, I'd like to play that piano," he said, pointing to one sitting to the side of the stage where he was about to walk off.

There was a great deal of discussion about the impossibility of him playing in the wings, with only muted light. It was decided that the piano would be moved to center stage.

It was done.

The boy sat down and began to play with sudden heaviness, scattering precise notes in fragments up and down the keyboard.

The students became fully alert.

The boy played on, not stopping, from one musical experience to the next. He played parts of some melodies, the whole of others, wandering in and out of them with persistent depth. There was fresh awe from the students. Some were silent, open-mouthed. They swayed and flowed in place, to his rhythm. They began to talk to him, calling to him with enthusiasm, encouraging, questioning. He ran deftly over the keys in beautiful arpeggios that rang clearly and confidently. He was at home at that piano and in that auditorium as if he and the students had reached a natural, unspoken understanding, as if all knew that, of course, he belonged there.

"Do you know 'Evil Woman?' " someone yelled out.

He kept on playing and answered as an aside, and softly, but I couldn't hear. Three or four times, he was asked about "Evil Woman." He was hunched, preoccupied, over the keys, playing with concentration and spontaneity.

Finally, he began "Evil Woman." His fingers plunged emphatically, deep within the keys, making the rock sounds precise and visible. The students sang along, enunciating the words, their heads swaying, their eyes misty. Others studied him.

When he was done, the group applauded eagerly, and, without stopping, he flowed into another tune. The students moved obviously now. Bodies swung and swayed in place; they clapped silently and limply to his rhythm. Random notes began anew and then "Hungarian Rhapsody" arose deeply. Switching mood and rhythm, his posture remained the same, hunched intensely over the keys, studying them closely, fingers flying rapidly.

The music came out of him, floated into the shadows and hard lights, swirled and echoed around and around the auditorium.

He began something else again, melding into it, and its newness, the reaching of another height, released something deep inside me all at once. That nameless, unrelenting hanging-on to the everyday worry of life was gloriously wrenched. My heart eased and was separated from my body: up, up, up, fluttering with his notes throughout the grand hall.

"Are you a concert pianist?" someone asked hesitantly.

I didn't hear his answer. I don't think he gave one. He was involved in his playing. He *was* the music.

"Are you *sure* you're not a concert pianist--? Aren't you someone famous?"

No answer.

The bell rang. That ugly, long, guttural, gravelly bell, ending the period. It jutted above the melody. The melody lingered heavily but brightly, and flitted around, then hugged the hard lights. He kept on and on.

Some students got up and walked away reluctantly to their next classes. Some just stood, watching, mesmerized. Most stayed and sat, hugging their knees or leaning on their hands against the floor of the platform.

I lingered, eventually rising, for I had another class. His music went on as I began to leave.

My heart was full: I felt young. I was happy, almost delirious.

As I went back through the curtained tunnel I had entered, the notes began to fade. They tinkled in my ears, and followed me, even after I was back in the harsh noisy reality of the halls once again.

The day ended after the next class, and when I walked to my car in the parking lot, I felt the spacious, sunny warmth all around. The gravel reflected the fullness of the sun and the brightness rose and spread, onto the tops of cars, into the dangling, fanning maple leaves. It was the first of many warm, spring days that would hint of summer, casting away the bitter winter we had just come through, giving us hope and something to look forward to.

Child Psychology-1:00

THE ASSIGNMENT: OBSERVE A CHILD IN A CLASSROOM OR SOCIAL setting. My next-door neighbor, three-years-old, was perfect. All summer she had been ringing my doorbell daily to spend time with me. She had chosen me as her friend; there was nothing fake or forced in the setup for the study. It was already a natural situation, relaxed and happy.

Janessa has an eight-year-old brother and a thirteen-year-old sister. Her father is a bookkeeper at a suburban nursing home and her mother is a nutritionist at a veteran's hospital in the city.

Her parents came to the United States from Manila, the Philippines, where, besides having established curfews, the government is suspected of having her mother's brother killed as he was arriving home with a friend on an evening out.

Her visits fill our home with delightful curiosity; sweet, intelligent questions urge firm and detailed answers. She dances whenever she feels like it: up and down the stairs, the stepladder in the kitchen, and her entrances and exits over the threshold of the front door as I open it for her. She is so free, and yet, at once a person of shyness and drama.

She follows me from room to room. From the start, she was intrigued by our eight cats, especially Fletcher, a large gray tabby with a raccoon-like tail. She lies on her stomach and puts her arms around him while he sleeps on the floor.

She is in play school three mornings a week, in the elementary school on the other side of her house. Her mother is concerned that she lapses into "baby talk."

The bell rings. Already, as I open the door, Janessa is smiling dreamily, her head back, her posture erect as a soldier's.

"Are you busy?"

She steps in over the threshold. Now her eyes are cautious and transfixed on my face.

"What's that on your nose?"

"It's medicine. I had a pimple." I wipe it away with a tissue.

"There's nothing there now."

"What pretty shoes!"

Caution vanishes. She points her toe, meaning for me to tie her shoe.

She declares, "I want to go to Berman's," which is a pharmacy a half-block away. She opens up her red jacket and pumps out her chest to show me what she is wearing, then spreads her hands on her waist.

"I have Strawberry Shortcake shirt."

Nearby, at the short stairway, she walks up joyously, holding onto the railing and mocking her own steps, her knees jutting out, then propping them forward to point her toes.

"See?"

She is asking for approval after I have shown her how to climb the stairs without sliding her hand onto the opposite wall as she did when she first came to visit.

Just before we enter the bedroom, I ask, "Did you have your hair cut?"

She nods firmly, her bob shaking into place.

Espying Fletcher on a pillow on the bed, she jumps on it, seat first, then crawls toward him as I sit on the edge. At first, he moves toward me, but he stays put as she carefully strokes his tail, looking up at me, smiling.

As Jerry comes in from outside, we hurry back downstairs, where he greets her. In the kitchen, as she sits in the chair, he admires her hair. Again, she shakes her head, and stretches to put her elbows on the table.

Pop! She is up!

"Look what I'm doing!"

Climbing the stepladder, her head high, she then goes back down quickly, tiptoeing all the way.

Fletcher has followed us and can be seen stretched out on the dining room table nearby. She watches him from the doorway, then recites in baby talk:

"I want to get little kitties so I can carry them. I want a little kitty so I can carry them."

Looking down, shyly, she says, "I love going to Berman's."

Skipping now around the kitchen. "Did you hear what Twinki (one of our other cats) said?"

"What?"

"Meow."

Jerry comments that her nose is "so cute--small and soft."

Distracted, with three fingers, she rubs her nose. I ask her if she is doing that because Jerry gave her a compliment. Shaking her head, making her hair fluffy again.

"Something's in it."

In unison, we ask, "Do you want a Kleenex?"

Again, she shakes her head. She seems sad.

"I want to go to Berman's. I want to buy enough Chiclets for all my friends: blue, red, orange. Enough for Christina and for me and my brother."

A man is walking by the front of our house, carrying a baby in a papoose on his back.

"Look, Janessa! Look out the window!"

Stilled in place, she twists her body, refusing to move. I implore her. At the window, she balances on tiptoe, fascinated at what she sees.

"Did you ever see that before?"

"No."

Outside, Roxie, another cat, bangs on the door with his paws to come in.

"Did he ring the bell?"

She swings her head from shoulder to shoulder, looking down at the cord of her jacket.

"I'm going to cry."

"Why?"

With teeth clenched and her lips loose, in baby talk, she says, "I'm afraid to go home becuz I won't go to Berman's."

I hug her and say that I will get dressed and take her there now.

The door downstairs opens; Janessa runs upstairs to the bedroom, jumps onto the floor with two feet in unison in front of me as I sit on the bed.

"I didn't stop; I just came right in."

She smiles her teeth-clenched smile.

"Look at my new shoes."

I request to see the backs. She turns, then moves her ankles sideways, while chewing gum in large, rhythmic chews, loud and juicy.

Fletcher is stilled on the bed as she throws herself onto him, then hugs him.

"He's not afraid of me."

Jumping back onto the floor, straightening up, she bends in a deep plié, then looks at me.

"Do squirrels go in trees in the winter?"

She adds, "Are you wearing your pajamas?"

"Yes."

"Why don't you wear pants?"

"When I grew up to be a lady, I decided to wear gowns."

Wide-eyed, she leans forward as I show her all the items in the closet; after I do, she touches each one delicately. She turns to the tray on the dresser nearby and points to a tiny perfume bottle among others.

"This is the cutest, the smallest."

She sits in a chair under the window, still chewing her gum.

"I go swimming in the pool, the baby pool, 'cause I'm afraid of the big pool. I go with my friends, Jessica and Christina. I always go under. I don't have goggles. When I grow big, I'm going in the big pool."

A set of small family photographs on a shelf above the chair catches her attention, and she turns to stare at them, then giggles.

"Your hair isn't curly. How did it used to be made straight?"

"I had it set in the beauty shop in large rollers."

Her knees folded under her, she giggles a little more and taps her fingertips on her nose as if she is playing the piano.

Janessa's brother comes to the front door to see if she is here. She runs to see him, then comes back upstairs to sit back on the chair and crosses her legs, her feet barely over the edge.

Going to the dresser, she lifts the tiny bottle gingerly off the tray, and asks, "Can I put on the perpyume?"

Just then, Jerry enters: "Say it right."

"Perfume."

Dotting her index finger on each wrist, she carefully traces the aroma all around; then, behind her ears, turning her head each way; on the center of her neck as she lifts her head; all with a dramatic expression on her face. Then, sweetly, she puts the tiny perfume bottle back on the mirrored oval tray framed in brassy lace.

"You--should put it on. Do this--," she tells me, rubbing her wrists together at nose level. She lifts a spray bottle off the tray, thrusts her arm toward me and leans against the side of the bed.

“”You put it right on me.”

I spray as she turns her head sideways and then she offers me the other arm, her head turning to the opposite direction.

“I love you,” she says in mumbled shouts, flopping back and forth on the edge of the bed.

“What?” I smile, eager, and lean toward her.

“I love you,” she mumbles again.

“Did you say, ‘I love you?’ ”

I touch her hand. Smiling widely, she pulls it away.

“Yes,” still bouncing away, back and forth against the bed.

“I love you, too.”

“I do apple jacks.” She leaps on and off the bed in belly flops. “I can’t do it.”

She reaches across the bed and grabs a lint roller, winding it up and down and sideways all over the bed, on her clothes, her back, her knees, her chest, her face.

“It’s on my nose, in my eyes, from the cats.”

“Let’s go in the yard,” my friend, Janessa, decides.

I follow her outside.

From Here: Looking Back, Remembering

The Bridge

Circa 1949

"The Bridge is up!"

That was the cry of excitement on a sweet summer day.

Automobiles began lining up tightly, then suddenly there were stilled rows of them, shimmering, waiting. Here and there, parents and children began scattering across the paralyzed boulevard to the stone balustrade over the Chicago River, the children smacking their palms against the granite, lost in ecstatic laughter.

There was a thin, tall man in a white short-sleeved shirt, the back heavily wrinkled from his leaning against the flannel of the driver's seat of his car for so long on a summer day. He bent down stiffly to pick up one of the little boys; up, the little head rose, higher than his own, and the small arm curled 'round his father's neck, the baby's other arm outstretched to dreamily watch his fingertips dancing across imaginary dots of air. Then the man turned halfway with his son in his arms, and they stared across the river, and waited along with his older son standing close by his side.

My father decided to wait no longer. He stepped out, and placed the crook of his arm atop the slice of half-opened door of our car, smiling faintly into the clear blue sky, surveying the cool summer afternoon with its clean, crisp breeze coming from the unseen spot where the lake and the river cross.

We could hear the groan of the foghorn. My mother and I scrambled out and the three of us rushed to where the crowd was lined up against the railing. We came up just in time to watch a sleek ship silently gliding through the river, a red band all around its rim and its mast valiantly upright within the wind. All along on the floor of the ship there were sailors wearing narrow black uniforms and black berets, each with a small red ball on top, with clear hard eyes waving eagerly, so much so that we longed to be with them; we were close enough to see that some had empty gaps between their teeth, making their smiles especially foreign and comical.

"They're French sailors," my father said. "The ship came all the way from France!"

There were huge wooden bobbins on the ship's floor, with enormous ropes and wires strung around them, and large iron machinery that we could not identify.

Smoothly, it swept under us, under the bridge, and we turned around and ran back through the tight spaces between the parked cars to reach the other side as the tip of the bow emerged, now, closer to us. The ship was near and large for moments, then diminished lazily, unstoppable, farther and farther into the horizon until at last the sailors became tiny dark figures.

Back in our car, we watched the mighty bridge come down directly in front of us: the mammoth breadth of cement, the wide white lines, the huge area of mesh that now locked onto Michigan Avenue, making the boulevard flat and approachable and ordinary once again. The huge steel girders bobbed and pounded and synchronized, closing with a roar.

I became giddy with the fantasy of danger: Had we been trapped while the bridge had been going up, we would have lost control of our very selves, rolling erratically and wildly down the pavement.

A car's motor roared; then, one by one, there were staccato-like echoes of it, while other cars mildly hummed into readiness. The bridge's rims locked in place. In front, the wooden bars lifted, swung open.

We turned our heads, our eyes lingering one last time toward the ship retreating into the light sky. I leaned back just slightly enough so that the breeze coming through the back window made my long hair flicker for an instant. Our car slowly gained momentum. To my delight, we drove on through the exact space where the bridge had so recently risen, having made it only a moment ago impossible to pass through it.

Today

I WAS STANDING IN THAT HESITANT MOMENT, JUST BEFORE LEAVING, near the door. I was about to lean toward it, even, and pull it open as I faced the young man behind the counter. We had said all the nice customer-clerk things (and I *enjoyed* that), he had given me my change, I was clutching my package. He gazed at me with lazy eyes from behind the cash register, shelves of film and cigarettes behind him. I returned his look.

"Did Frank's wife have her baby yet?"

It is *that* kind of drug store, an old-fashioned, friendly neighborhood place, on a corner next to a short line of other stores; even the linoleum floor, patterned like traditional old brick, has remained. Frank is one of the owners; his wife was already two weeks late.

"No," he answered, matter-of-factly.

"That's difficult," I offered, without being asked, and then I explained, "I was *early* with *mine* and it was *hard*---I can imagine how hard it must be for *her*."

He shrugged his shoulders.

Suddenly, I *felt* the child inside me. There was the growing baby *inside*. The heart beating thickly, softly. The cream-baby skin. The wandering infinitesimal veins. The strings of healthy blood. The clouds of misunderstood emotion, heavily weighted, filling me up. My whole inside, weighing me down, scraping the ground in tight-heat August. The tingling on my fingertips, the lines of water-dots along the insides of my fingers, all summer long. The heavy space behind my eyes. The water-sadness a necklace dipping across my throat, tingling just below my ears. My eyes drowsy; dots dancing inside my forehead. Sleep. I could sleep forever.

It took seconds to feel this, but all he saw was this: a careful toss of the head, a pleasant smile, and a steady, "Goodbye, see you tomorrow." I pulled the door open, and went outside.

There was dull lead across my chest. I began the block-and-a-half walk home. There was the day breathing, the leaves rustling and swaying greatly overhead, making dark and fuzzy shades on the bright, pale-yellow street. There were the small, lovely, lonely homes set far back on either side.

And I remembered as I walked: my silken breasts, warm, thick, bulging, brushing exquisitely along the gauze lining of my light sleeveless dress. I am sitting on the wooden bench, cradling my newborn daughter, looking down at her inside the lap of my pleated skirt, my chin on my throat. The gray lady sits at the other end of the park bench, her head tilted and her eyes lukewarm, suspicious. I wonder at her past.

I have taken the baby out of the buggy, into the summer air and am giving her the first water bottle outdoors. I am a mother, grandly shy.

It is cool under the canopies of leaves, in the secret shades near the barks of trees, and warm where the sun splays across the grass, the heat breathing, reaching me. I face the lake. Hair strands interrupt across the bridge of my nose and into my eyes, and I blink them away. The breeze is full and swift now and then, across my face. Summer is in balance, perfectly.

Today, the pavements are bright all the way home. I put the key in the lock, turn it, juggling the package, and go inside. I close the door. There is a deeper darkness, air- conditioned. I am home.

Mid Afternoon in Winter
4-11-93
RWM

RWM
8-9-80

Our Baby Grand Piano

My father died this past year, and my mother is planning to move into a much smaller apartment than she lives in now, so the baby grand piano that I grew up with just will not fit into her new place. It will not fit into our suburban tri-level house, either, and, besides, we live with several cats who would most likely lust after its glossy wood veneer as their own tree house and scratching post.

There is splendor in the silken finish of our baby grand piano, the color of caramel, with muted baroque carvings flowing downward onto each of the three curvaceous legs, so that the limbs and the leafy embellishments are one.

From the beginning, our piano was situated in a comfortable corner of our small living room, in front of a slender upright French window that opened and closed like a little door and looked out onto the wide steps of the courtyard and the sidewalk beyond.

I would pull the matching wooden bench closer to the window sill, sit and tuck my knee under me, feeling the late afternoon as I watched the stillness of it, often after having whisked down the sidewalk toward Broadway on a spring day with the only purpose being to take in the newly reborn air that always lifted me.

When the piano tuner came, the huge kidney-shaped cover was flung open as the brass rod held it aloft, exposing the hallowed space underneath that cradled the angelic sounds. I watched the grace of his fingertips lifting ever so slightly the taut strings, rearranging the tones back into place.

The piano could delight in unexpected ways, not just for us. There were my friends and I in a circle, holding hands, dancing and singing in the living room, "Here we go luby loo, here we go luby li, here we go luby loo-o---all on a Saturday night!"

Aunt Helen, in her schoolteacher way, was accompanying us on our piano, nails clicking, fingers fleeing swiftly and deftly over the keys, her head swaying to the perfect linear rhythm she was creating as though she were dancing with us; eyes, framed by horned-rimmed glasses, set at attention toward the sheet in front of her on the stand.

It seemed that having such a masterful instrument of music was entirely my father's idea. He took naturally to the piano, and I wondered about the gene he must have inherited. Without straining, he played, "We're Loyal to You, Illinois," and "Cheer, Cheer, for old Notre Dame," and "Go U Northwestern," all easily rising out of the magic of the college song book of maroon leather bound in a golden spine.

After coming back home from my first two summer months at overnight camp when I was ten, I mourned lake and sky and sunshine over the hill that oozed green dew after being mowed and the trees that sloped all the way down to the bottom of it, where the pier went on into the lake where we learned to swim.

At the end of August, looking sadly out the corner window with the piano at my back, I relived my refusal to go into the water for the first month of the camp season, watching the swimming counselors teaching my cabin mates. And then, one day, I just went in. As days went by, I swam eagerly near the shore, while catfish circled us, their large heads sprouting whiskers, and I, now, unafraid, delighted.

When I was twelve, I began taking lessons. Mrs. Lewis was a nice person with piano-teacher fingernails: short enough, but not too short, so as not to clack on the keys and break, rounded nicely at the ends, stopping just beyond the fingertips, painted in slightly-darkened, piano-teacher red. I watched as she demonstrated placement of the hands: wrists low, under the edge, fingers cupped, placed evenly a little above the row of keys, with the note of C centered between. She did this to perfection.

I took joy in this new phase of learning, being able to magically transform new symbols named with single capitalized letters into notes that came to life as music.

I practiced dutifully, at least half-an-hour every day, while my mother cleared her throat every now and then as she tiptoed around in the dining room nearby, thinking she was unnoticed and unobtrusive. I learned to play the easy versions of, "The Sabre Dance," with its startling staccato rhythm, and ultimately the deepened, emotion-producing strokes of "Rhapsody in Blue." Mrs. Lewis was content with my performances and so was I.

Two productive years passed by, and at the end of June, prior to my going to two months of overnight camp right before my freshman year of high school, Mrs. Lewis pointed to grids spaced above the rows of notes on the opened sheet music of my latest exercise. In her low voice she announced that I would learn chords next semester, which I took as a gentle promise, and further, as encouragement of my ability to understand music.

However, my fourteen-year-old spirit and my body awoke to tempt me in other ways. A growing social life consumed me, and I let my piano learning experience drift away.

During my freshman year in college, a family trust came to fruition, allowing us to move into a new high-rise apartment building, one of the very first of a brand new era of modern architecture in Chicago. On the corner of Sheridan Road and Belmont Avenue, where my friends and I had played games when it was just open space, it faced the Outer Drive and Belmont Harbor. Now, taking an elevator high up to the fourteenth floor, we had to get used to walking back and forth on soon-to-be-carpeted floors made of concrete, giving us headaches; the unending swishing sounds rising from streams of colorful automobiles on the Drive; at night, the lights of lampposts and front lights of cars sweeping and twinkling against the blackness; a large living room with a window spanning the entire wall, so that the sailboats strewn on the waters of the Harbor were an image that we could look at whenever we wanted. An entirely new way of living for us, here now was a life of luxury, as though we had arrived inside an eternal vacation.

The Baby Grand Piano was now set off to a side in front of the sweeping window of the large living room, lost, isolated. The bench was replaced by a copied Louis XIV chair, cushioned, and, at the insistence of the decorator, positioned out and slightly away from the piano keys.

Years later, in the airy living room near the window that spanned the entire wall, my father would take out the maroon songbook and play the college fight songs as he did when I was growing up; only now, without even looking at the sheet music, he would be chuckling and pretending to be a suave professional, showing off for my two daughters, who would be leaning against the side of the keys.

Today, a piano dealer who, with his innate passion for the beauty of music finely tuned, is begging my mother to let him buy our Baby Grand. As my mother explains her dilemma in making a decision, I can actually feel his reverence for it. I am tortured by the certainty of what will happen, instead: our treasure being handed over to her best friend's daughter-in-law, at an unforgivably low price. My agony is furthered by the hurt that the person receiving it has caused by her purposeful alienation from our family.

And so, I am bereft by the undeniable loss of the Baby Grand Piano I grew up with, only comforted somewhat by having learned from Mrs. Lewis that the names of the notes on the lines of the upper staff can be recognized by remembering that: Every Good Boy Does Fine.

My Heart

Blue Jeans

SHE STANDS WITHIN THE REFLECTION OF THE LIGHT THAT BEAMS through the window from outside, a dull light, light of late afternoon that glows against her face, while her eyes are gazing through it. She is in front of a circular chrome pants rack that displays blue jeans, staring at the volumes of them presented to her, the vast selection. It is this way each time she cannot cope: She goes to the pants store to look at blue jeans.

'Why does everything seem impossible, unsolvable? Why does everything wrong and strange happen to me? My friends don't have these problems, why me? Why am I so different, so jumpy, so restless? I can't concentrate, I can't sit still. I reach, I try, but I get nowhere. Oh, how I try.'

Now, her back faces me as we wait in the doctor's examining room. Everything is going well, at least for now, in that suspended space where time passes and where nothing happens, and that is good, because all is calm.

From behind her, I see her smooth hair shining with dark blonde luster, sculpted close to her head, ending gently just below her neck in an uplift as she tilts her head.

"I can remember when I was younger," she murmurs.

Her arms, where I cannot see, are embraced in front of her on the desk around a book of matches, which she twiddles within her fingertips.

"--I never had any problems--I never had to worry--. Everything was nice when I was young--."

Her voice is low.

Now, I know--. Although I cannot see, tears are brimming inside the rims of her eyes, one running swiftly down her silken cheek to mar it.

"I never thought it would be like this--I never knew--. I was always happy--content--I had fun--I liked everything I did--."

Still twisting the matches, bending them unmercifully, she yanks them out of their container and turns back slightly, throwing them onto the desk behind her. She swivels around so that she is facing me, now. Yes, the red veins are a net over the bulging whites around her large blue eyes.

'See? I am a human being, after all. I am a person who cares. I care, very much.'

She almost smiles.

"Why is he taking so long? I have so many things to do."

"He'll be here soon," I reassure her, not really knowing, but comforting us both. "We will be out of here soon, and we'll have a nice dinner, you'll see."

"Can Shari eat over?" she asks, the sudden idea pleasing her.

"Oh, yes! Of course."

She takes a deep breath, shaking her arm slightly. Her eyes meander around the familiar room and on up over the ceiling.

"It's cold--. I'm cold."

"In a moment the doctor will be back, and the test will be over and you can put your blouse back on. Just be patient."

We stare simply toward each other, and then look at the things around the room in our own separate ways: the baby scale, the sink with the foot pedal, the chart that hangs from a string on the door, the balloon-printed wallpaper, the clear canister of cotton balls. I am restless, too, now, and wish to go.

We lean to one another, and kiss; and I begin to cry, with gladness, because I will never stop hoping.

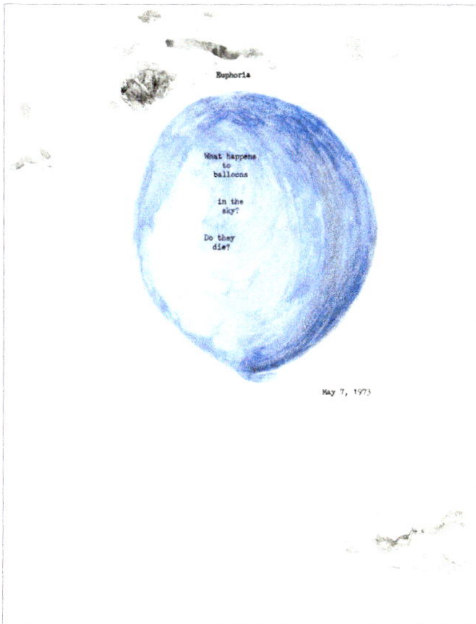

Photographs of Images by Guy Nicol

CPSIA information can be obtained at www.ICGtesting.com
Printed in the USA
BVOW11s2140050215

386206BV00014B/35/P

9 781629 011516